PIETY
AND
PERSEVERANCE

Jews from the Carpathian Mountains

PIETY AND PERSEVERANCE

Jews from the Carpathian Mountains

by
HERMAN DICKER

Foreword by
ELIE WIESEL

SEPHER-HERMON PRESS, INC.
New York

PIETY AND PERSEVERANCE

Library of Congress Cataloging in Publication Data

Dicker, Herman, 1914-
    Piety and perseverence.

    Bibliography: p.
    Includes index.
    1. Jews--Ukraine--Zakarpatskaia oblast'--History.
2. Jews--Romania--Sighetu Marmaţiei--History. 3. Holocaust, Jewish (1939-1945)--Ukraine--Zakarpatskaia
oblast'. 4. Holocaust, Jewish (1939-1945)--Romania--
Sighetu Marmaţiei. 5. Hasidism--Ukraine--Zakarpatskaia
oblast'. 6. Hasidism--Romania--Sighetu Marmaţiei.
7. Zakarpatskaia oblast' (Ukraine)--Ethnic relations.
8. Sighetu Marmaţiei (Romania)--Ethnic relations.
I. Title.
DS135.R93Z273   940'.04924   80-54595
ISBN 0-87203-094-6   AACR2

To the Memory
of
My Parents

FOREWORD

This book is close to my heart. It illuminates a universe that was mine, and which is no more. Swept away in the storm, the Jewish universe of the Carpathians. Buried beneath the ashes of history.

One must read this work—at the same time scholarly and journalistic—in order to rediscover the Jewish communities gone up in smoke: how alive, how captivating they were, those Jewish communities of Sighet and Satmar, of Munkács and Wizhnitz! With their rabbis and their poets, their sages and their dreamers, they surpassed in vigor, in creative imagination, in hope as well, all that is found in a society at first in process of formation, and afterwards, destruction.

Products of history, they seemed to evolve outside of the events that were taking place in the world far away. The great upheavals on the other side of the mountains only barely affected them. And yet, there were some little known points of contact: how many people know that the famous Rabbi Meir Berlin had come to Sighet in 1928 to participate in a Mizrahi conference? Fewer still are aware of the fact that the illustrious humorist Hersh-Leib Gottlieb had paid a visit to Theodore Herzl, and that he had convinced the leader of the Zionist movement to obtain Hebrew type for his Zionist review, published in his native city of Sighet.

Those cities, so poor, so cold, where the Jews were building their dream kingdoms: the Hassidim were against the
Mitnagdim, the Zionists were battling with their adversaries
who were preaching patience and repentance ... All these
conflicts, all these debates between orthodox and neologs,
adherents of Satmar and of Wizhnitz, are found again in these
pages. Moreover, we learn the way the Jews studied, prayed,
and survived. We weep over the poverty of the wandering
beggars, and we are carried away by their song. What did
these communities do to overcome despair? How did they
succeed in invoking joy, individual and collective joy, when
all around them, their enemies were sharpening their knives?
How can we explain such fervor within men and women so
threatened? How can we comprehend their wish to build
homes, centers of study, schools, when their world was about
to collapse in darkness? How can we explain the inexplic-
able? The author of this work, Herman Dicker, does not even
try, and we must be grateful to him for that. He only reports
what he has gleaned. A searcher, he provides us with the
fruits of his research. Guided by him, the reader strolls in the
regions under the spell of Jewish geography—and Jewish
memory—and there, comes face to face with a past, impreg-
nated with glory and sadness, grandeur and melancholy.

To be sure, as happens often, the historian is sometimes
mistaken. The Seer of Lublin could not have been the faithful
disciple of the Besht—and was not; Gershom Scholem is
known as a great interpreter of mystical, and not Hassidic
thought. And then, may the author forgive me, I did not
completely recognize myself in the somewhat too-glowing
portrait that with good intentions he has painted of me: the
Kingdom of Night, appears—unfortunately—only in a small
number of my writings. So as not to risk desecrating it, I have
preferred to turn towards other places, other themes, other
times.

No matter, these are errors of detail. We may then continue. What counts is the cumulation of facts and their di-

versity: we observe the Jews of the Carpathians from every angle. What counts is the total view. The author shares with us his, which is vast and panoramic, and at the same time, personal. A military chaplain in the American Army during the Second World War, he relates his dramatic, poignant encounters with the Jewish survivors in Occupied Germany and Austria. It is through their eyes that he glimpses the story of their common past.

The communities that he brings to life had been flourishing, at times dazzling: Hassidic dynasties since the Besht, Hebrew schools, philanthropic activities, reports of the "Joint," publications in Yiddish, movements of cultural emancipation, of social disputes and religious obstinacy . . . the Talmudic scholar, the enterprising businessman, the wedding jester, the tough and hardened peasants. In barely two centuries, this mountainous region had produced a highly colorful society, touching and fascinating, throbbing with life and faith, so much so that one believed it would last forever.

It is, therefore, not surprising that Herman Dicker speaks of it with love. His nostalgia is contagious.

Elie Wiesel

CONTENTS

ILLUSTRATION CREDITS

R. Abramovitch, *The Vanished World,* © Forward Association, New York, 1947, 1, 2, 3, 4, 10.
R. Vishniak, *Polish Jews,* © Schocken Books, Inc., New York, 1947, 8, 9.
Central Archives and Research Institute for the History of Gedolei Yisrael, Jerusalem, 7.
YIVO Institute, New York, 12, 13, 14.
M. Lubetsky Film and Photo Collection, Jerusalem, 18.
Isaac Geld, 19, 20, 21.
N.Y. Daily News, 22.
Joseph Kahan, 23.

INTRODUCTION

While I was growing up in Stuttgart, Germany, in the 1920's, I could scarcely have imagined that fifty years later I would be writing about Jews from the Carpathian Mountains. I knew that I had been born there, in a little village called Körösmezö, when it still belonged to Hungary; and I remembered the time when my father, of blessed memory, took me along on his annual visit to his family. But beyond that, I knew very little, and perhaps was not too keen on finding out. Since my place was Germany, it was here where I hoped to build a future for myself.

Still, as time went by, I began to realize that I was an alien in this German environment. My birthplace had, after World War I, become a part of Czechoslovakia, which made me a Czech citizen living abroad. Then, when Hitler started to cast his shadow upon the land, I decided to enroll at the German University of Prague, Czechoslovakia, only to discover that I had to pass a Czech language proficiency test in order to be admitted. Since learning Czech would have taken too much of my time, I traveled to Berlin where I spent four years at the Hildesheimer Rabbinical Seminary and the State University. When at last I submitted my dissertation on medieval history, I was told by the Nazi dean that it was "inadequate." My angry professor, a renowned scholar in medieval history, recommended me to his colleague at the University of Zurich, Switzerland. There I obtained my doctorate with the identical dissertation, and with the degree of magna cum laude.

A fortuitous affidavit enabled me to enter the United States. Soon, I found myself in the uniform of a United States Army Chaplain, on duty with an infantry division preparing for combat on the battlefields of Europe. These were dramatic years, particularly when our division helped liberate the concentration camps of Nazi Germany. I learned firsthand the grim story of the Holocaust, during which my own parents and many members of my family were murdered.

Years later—I had already retired from the army—while talking about family and tradition at a Passover seder, one of my brothers asked, "If I don't even know where I come from, what can I transmit to my children?" This remark challenged me to start collecting all available information on our family, researching deep into the nineteenth century. Ultimately, it led to a publication entitled, "A Jewish Family Trail: the Dickers and Their Mates," which was published early in 1977. Although well received, I felt that much more needed to be written; there had to be many more whose roots derived from the same region and who had scant knowledge about the lives of their ancestors. I found that the region of Subcarpathian Ruthenia, once with over 100,000 Jews, had been politically and economically deprived, but spiritually strong and vibrant. In the course of more than 300 years, it had produced great rabbis and flourishing communities. Then suddenly, in a few short weeks of 1944, all these human riches were gone, destroyed in the ovens of Auschwitz.

As a frontline chaplain of the American army, it was my privilege to aid many Holocaust victims. I was always astonished at their ability to start life anew; more than that, I was constantly amazed at how the survivors, many of Hasidic background, not only tried, but succeeded in continuing their life style here in the United States.

Thus, I made it my goal to trace the historical development of the region, describing the political, social and economic conditions of these 100,000 Jewish men, women and children. In order to bring their story closer, I have included poignant expressions of the people themselves: how they lived; how they sang; how they suffered and perished and how some survived.

None of this came easily, for while I was born in the region, I grew up in Germany, far removed from the social milieu of Subcarpathian Ruthenia. Thus, this book represents a sort of self-discovery and, to a larger extent, a memorial to past generations. In addition, it will acquaint us with the survivors of the Holocaust, and provide a bridge to better understanding of some Hasidic communities in the United States.

Fortunately, my efforts were assisted by many, too many to enumerate. However, there are some who deserve special mention: foremost among them is Professor David Weiss Halivni of the Jewish Theological Seminary, whose prodigious memory was an inspiring source in my research. He introduced me to Elie Wiesel who has graced my efforts with a compassionate Foreword. Dr. Arnon Yardeni, another native of the Carpathian Mountains, helped me with many details. Professor Paul Robert Magocsi of the Harvard Ukrainian Institute whose own *Shaping of a National Identity: Subcarpathian Rus' 1848-1948*, served as the major reference of the region's general history. Dr. Bernard J. Mandelbaum, Executive Vice President, Synagogue Council of America, provided warm and continuous encouragement throughout. The Hebrew University Library of Jerusalem, the Joint Archives of New York and the Jewish Theological Seminary Library yielded much primary source material. To all these institutions and their staffs, I am much indebted. There were also many interviews with scholars, survivors of the Holocaust and knowledgeable individuals whose contributions enhanced the character of this story.

Additionally, I derived much financial and moral support from the Littauer and Jensam foundations and the National Foundation for Jewish Culture. The same holds true for the Cracow Friendship Society, Mr. Sam Rosentool of blessed memory, colleagues, relatives and friends, especially Mr. Irwin Gelbart whose generosity made possibile the simultaneous publication of a paperback edition.

Heartfelt appreciation is also in order to Jane Salodof for her sensitive editorial advice and Samuel Gross, the most diligent editor-publisher, whose efforts helped shape this volume into its present form.

Finally, in a category all by itself, is my family. Words are inadequate to describe the tireless contribution of Eileen, my devoted partner. At all times she was prepared to yield her own busy schedule to the never ending demands of the manuscript. As for Anna and Eli, our beloved children, they each added their share to this family enterprise with enthusiasm and diligence.

Above all, I am grateful to the Almighty for allowing this labor of love to reach its fruition. May it serve as a memorial to the past and an inspiration to future generations.

PART I

THE HISTORY

Jewish communities in Hungary before 1918.

(From Hungarian Jewish Studies, Vol. I, New York, 1966. Courtesy World Federation of Hungarian Jews)

CZECHOSLOVAKIA

AUSTRIA

POLAND

U S S R

Y U G O S L A V I A

R U M A N I A

LIKA-KRBAVA
12

MODRUS-
FIUME
2,078

Zagrabo
(Zagreb)

ZAGRAB
5,680

BELOVAR-
KÖRÖS
2,406

POZSEGA
2,432

VERŐCE
5,199

SZEREM
3,779

Eszéko
(Osijek)

Ujvidek
(Novi Sad)

Zimony
(Zemun)

Pancsova
(Pancevo)

Versec
(Vrsac)

VARASD
1,341

Varasd
(Varazdin)

VAS
9,469

Szombathely

ZALA
12,892

Nagykanizsa
10,645

Keszthely

Zalaegerszeg

SOMOGY
10,645

Kaposvar

BARANYA
8,828

Pecs

Mohács

Bonyhad

TOLNA
8,159

Szekszard

Baja

SOPRON
8,192

Sopron
(Vaas)

VESZPREM
8,282

Papa

Veszprem

GYÖR
7,119

Györ
(Raab)

Komarom
(Komarno)

FEHER
7,382

Szekes-
feharvar

Esztergom
Vac

MOSON
881

Dunaszerdahely
(Dun.
Streda)

POZSONY
22,588

Pozsony
(Bratislava)

Szered
(Sered)

NYITRA
22,942

O Nyitra
(Nitra)
O Galanta
(Galanta)
Érsekujvár
(Nove
Zamky)
O Léva
(Levice)

BARS
4,969

HONT
3,180

PEST
245,157

Budapest

Ujpest
10,244

Kispest

Kiskörös

Nagykörös

Kecskemet

Cegled

PILIS-

Kiskunfelegyhaza

SOLT-

KISKUN
245,157

JASZ-NAGYKUN-
15,301

Jaszbereny

SZOLNOK
10,313

Szolnok

Törökszentmiklos

Karcag

Mezőtur

CSONGRAD
10,296

Szentes

Szeged

Hodmezovasarhely
77,444

Mako
3,353

CSANAD
3,353

BEKES
77,444

O Oroshaza

Bekescsaba

Szarvas

Gyula

BACS-BODROG
18,244

Szabadka
(Subotica)

Zenta
(Senta)

Nagykikinda
(Kikinda)

Nagybecskerek
(Zrenjanin)

TORONTAL
6,114

TEMES
9,733

Temesvar
(Timisoara)

KRASSO-
SZÖRENY
4,795

Lugos
(Lugoj)

Arad

ARAD
10,012

BIHAR
32,462

Nagyvarad
(Oradea)

Berettyoujfalu

HAJDU
15,301

Debrecen

Hajduboszormeny

Hajdunanas

HUNYAD
5,679

TRENCSEN
10,809

Trencsen
(Trencin)

ARVA
2,205

TUROC
1,981

O Turoc-szentmarton
(L. St. Mikulas)

Liptoszentmiklos

LIPTO
3,237

ZOLYOM
3,080

Besztercebanya
(Banska Bystrica)

Beszterce-
banya

GÖMÖR
5,603

Losonc
(Lucenec)

KISHONT

NOGRAD
9,461

Salgotarjan

Balassagyarmat

HEVES
18,346

Gyöngyös

Hatvan

Eger

BORSOD
18,346

Miskolc

Szikszo

ABAUJ-TORNA
14,251

Kassa
(Kosice)

SZEPES
7,475

Löcse
(Levoca)

Kesmark
(Kezmarok)

SAROS
12,323

Eperjes
(Presov)

O Bartfa
(Bardejov)

ZEMPLEN
33,041

Satoraljaujhely

Sarospatak

Sator-
aljaujhely

Tokaj

SZABOLCS
25,376

Nyiregyhaza

Nyirbator

Nagykallo

Kisvarda

Nyregyhaza

Mateszalka

Budszentmihaly

SZATMAR
29,468

Szatmarnemeti
(Satu-Mare)

Nagykaroly
(Carei)

UNG
17,587

Ungvar
(Uzhgorod)

BEREG
33,660

Munkacs
(Mukacevo)

Beregszasz
(Beregovo)

UGOCSA
11,850

Huszt
(Khust)

Nagyszöllös
(Vinogradov)

MARAMAROS
65,694

Maramarossziget
(Sighet)

Körösmező
(Yasinia)

Felsöviso
(Viseu-de-Sus)

Borsa

SZILAGY
9,849

Szilagysomlyo
(Simleu)

Zilah
(Zalau)

KOLOZS
12,561

Kolozsvar
(Cluj)

SZOLNOK-
DOBOKA
12,797

Des
(Dej)

BESZTERCE-
NASZOD
7,254

Beszterce
(Bistrita)

MAROS-
TORDA
7,550

Marosvasarhely
(Targu-Mures)

TORDA-
ARANYOS
2,648

ALSO-FEHER
3,845

Gyulafehervar-

KISKÜKÜLLÖ
1,766

NAGYKÜKÜLLÖ
1,089

UDVARHELY
1,313

CSIK
1,222

HAROMSZEK
905

BRASSO
2,357

Brasso
(Stalin)

FOGARAS
1,503

SZEBEN
1,565

Tisza R.

Danube R.

Danube R.

LEGEND:
- .... Boundary of county
- —·—·— International borders 1945
- BEKES — Name of county.
- 77,444 — Number of Jews in county, 1910
- ● Main community in 1910
- ○ 150—1,000 }
- ▲ 1,100—5,000 } Main communities in 1910 and within modern Hungary.
- ■ 95,000 — Population figures for 1946.

1. HUNGARIAN JEWS FROM THE 18th CENTURY TO WORLD WAR I

Our story, an important part of the general history of Central Europe, leads from the Kingdom of Hungary in the 18th century to modern Israel and the United States in our own day. Its focus is on the eastern Carpathian mountains, a geographical area divided and redivided between Hungary, Poland, Czechoslovakia, Rumania, Russia and, for a short but devastating time, Germany. Crucial movements—religious passion, emancipation, nationalism, war—mark the odyssey of its protagonists, a group of Jews who, at their peak, numbered more than 100,000 men, women and children.[1]

During the 16th and 17th centuries, Hungary had been dominated by the Turks and their Ottoman Empire. Then in 1699, the Austrian Habsburgs defeated the Turks, reuniting Hungary under their rule. Whereas Hungary's population had dwindled drastically under the Turks, the new rulers encouraged the immigration of large numbers of Slovaks, Serbs, Rumanians and Germans. This policy raised the population in the 18th century from 2½ to 8 million, making Hungary a state with many ethnic minorities, a situation that would cause never-ending problems in succeeding years. The same century also witnessed a sizable Jewish immigration, although on a much smaller scale. In the 1740's, there were approximately 20,000 Jews in all of Hungary, a number that increased to 80,000 by the end of the century.

From where did these Jewish immigrants originate? In

1

the main, they came from countries adjacent to Hungary and can be divided into three groups. First, there were the Austro-German Jews who joined their brethren in the western counties of Hungary, where most of the Jews had lived up to 1700. Then, there was an influx from the northeast, the Moravian-Bohemian Jews, whose immigration ended by 1770. These two groups dispersed rather quickly, moving from the border regions into the central and southern regions of the country. Third, there was the group, which originated from Galicia, the Polish province to the north. It is this wave, the largest of the three, and its history, with which we begin our story.

The Jews of Galicia had been escaping across the Carpathian mountains into Hungary since 1648, when murderous attacks under Chmelnitzki, the Cossak leader, killed hundreds of thousands of their brethren in Poland. The movement from Galicia became even stronger in 1772, when this province became a part of the Austro-Hungarian Empire, and Poland was partitioned between Austria, Russia and Prussia. At the time of partition, Galician Jewry numbered approximately 200,000, more than twice as many Jews as in all of Hungary.[2] A large number lived in the villages of Eastern Galicia. Their neighbors were the Ruthenians, an ethnic group whose history is greatly intertwined with the history of the Jews north and south of the Carpathian mountains. In Galicia the Jews had been living in abject poverty, particularly those who dwelled in small villages. They held leases, sold liquor and kept inns. They were the traders, to whom the Ruthenian peasants turned to sell their crops and to buy their meager supplies. When the Jews from Galicia moved south across the Carpathian mountains into northeasten Hungary, they found similar living conditions: Ruthenian peasants, small mountain villages and dire poverty. Still, they kept coming in the hope that Hungary would provide more living space and better economic opportunities in a more stable political setting.

What was the legal situation that confronted the immigrants in Hungary? It centered on those landlords who had received large estates from the king, the absolute head of the state and source of all power. The Jews had to pay taxes to the landlords on whose estates they settled and from whom they were supposed to receive protection. The largest estate owner in northeastern Hungary was the House of Schoenborn, from whose archives we learn that the Jews leased the right to mill flour as well as sell whisky and meat. We also read that they were engaged in the moving of lumber, the biggest natural treasure of these mountains, as far away as the great Baltic port of Danzig. Upon their return, they reported what they saw to Count Schoenborn who, in turn, transmitted their observations to the Imperial Court of Vienna.[3] From other sources we gather that Jews worked in the fields, raised cattle and were artisans. All in all, they had to work very hard to eke out a living for their families and pay the ever-increasing taxes. Their food was simple and homegrown. Bread was made of oats and maize; white bread was rare, baked only for the Sabbath and festive occasions. Living in isolated mountain villages, the Jews adopted many of the ways of their neighbors, the Ruthenian peasants. They wore fur hats and white woolen clothes in the winter; in the summer their children were covered with long white shirts. With spiritual guidance almost nonexistent, some Jews relaxed the strict observance of their religious customs. Others fell prey to the preachings of Jacob Frank (died 1791), a Jew from Podolia who claimed to be the Messiah and promised them salvation from their misery.

It was this simple and harsh mountain setting that provided the basis for a movement that deeply affects Jewish life to this very day. This movement is Hasidism. Its founder was Rabbi Israel ben Eliezer (1700-1760), better known as the Baal Shem Tov (Master of a Good Name), and his Hebrew initials, BESHT.[4] His birthplace has been traced to Okop, a suburb of Kolomea in Eastern Galicia. While much of Besht's early history is surrounded by legends, most scholars agree that the father of this modern movement of religious piety was influenced by his Carpathian mountain environs. His humble beginnings, his prolonged seclusion in the mountains and his passionate concern for humans and animals are all characteristic of an individual close to nature. In the stories reported about him, one scholar of folklore tries to see motifs similar to those of the Gentile Hutsuls, an ethnic group that lived in northeastern Hungary, southeastern Galicia and northern Bukovina.[5] Another theory, however, that the teachings of the Besht were directly influenced by the dissenting sects of the Russian Church[6] has been completely rejected by responsible researchers.[7] To quote the anthropologist Patai just briefly, "All the ecstatic exercises and antics, which the Hasidim seem to have adopted from the religious life of their Gentile neighbors are but *forms* of religious expression; the content they express is the same old Jewish belief in the God of our Fathers, which motivated the Jews since the days of Moses."[8] One might add that the preachings and the lifestyle of the Besht and his disciples only reemphasized the need "to serve God in joy" as prescribed by the psalmist of old. This accent on living, singing and dancing endeared the Besht initially to all the simple folk who had little education, but tried to find a way to serve God. It brought about a violent reaction by the established Jewish leaders, who advocated an approach to God through study and learning. They became known in history as the *Mitnagdim*, i.e. the opponents of Hasidism.

Our own story will show that this conflict continued throughout the 19th and 20th century, even though the Hasidic rabbis soon restored the need for study as an important ingredient of Jewish living. It will be seen that this blend of joyful living under God and minute observance of religious laws produced a strong sense of piety within the Hasidim; this enabled them to persevere in their lifestyle under the most adverse conditions. The Jews of our own story are prime examples of this piety and perseverance. The following pages will attempt to pinpoint their struggles, their defeats and their comebacks.

THE NORTHEASTERN COUNTIES
Bereg County and Munkács

The Hungarian Kingdom was divided into 63 counties. The four northeastern ones, Ung, Bereg, Ugocsa and Máramaros were all to the south of Galicia whence the majority of the immigrants came. We begin with the County of Bereg and its major city of Munkács because Jews already were recorded there from the middle of the 17th century.[9] At that time, Bereg County belonged to the estate of Count Rakóczy. In 1711, however, the estate was taken away from him by the Habsburg Emperor Leopold I and given to the Schoenborn family, whose first member, Count Lothar Franz Schoenborn, had been a bishop in Germany. He and succeeding members of this family did not live on the estate, but administered it from afar through local administrators. Jewish settlements developed slowly. The earliest statistics from Bereg County list five heads of households in 1700, 235 in 1735 and 1,460 in 1787. Although the country needed immigrants, Jewish settlers from Galicia were not readily welcomed by the Imperial authorities ruling in Vienna. They issued several edicts designed to stem the flow of immigrants from the north. One of these reveals their anti-Jewish thinking quite openly, exclaiming: "Lest they exploit His Majesty's inhabitants of the true faith." Fortunately, the local administrators of the Schoenborn estates were less prejudiced and more practical. They needed the Jewish immigrants to lease their concessions and to sell their produce. As their major concern was to increase the income from the estate, they availed themselves of the Jews' services, which proved more productive than those of non-Jews. This attitude became quite evident in 1768 when the Jews of Munkács asked Count Schoenborn for permission to build a synagogue. In granting this request, he stipulated that the Munkács Jews invite their fellow religionists from Galicia to settle on the Schoenborn estates.

When it came to taxes, both national and local authorities had one interest in common: to try to obtain as much from the Jews as possible. This often created a conflict between national and local powers at the expense of the Jewish taxpayers who were caught in-between. There was a whole variety of taxes: a *Toleranz* (protection) tax, a head tax, a land tax and an animal tax. Jewish innkeepers were told to report on suspicious guests. We also hear of an Israel Lazarovits who, in 1742, was sent to Poland to purchase war material for the troops of Empress Maria Theresa (1740-1780). In many ways the Jews were used and, in turn, let themselves be used to strengthen their economic and social position in the land.

By the end of the century there were enough Jews in Munkács to warrant the services of a communal rabbi. The first one recorded was Abraham Gottesman who served from 1790 until 1814. Besides being the local leader, he also functioned as the chief rabbi of the entire County of Bereg. To help him with his duties, he had a *Bet Din* (religious court) whose members, the *Dayanim* (judges) adjudicated the day-by-day cases in the life of the community. In addition, there was the group of *Parnasim*, best described as elders whose principal function was the assessment and collection of the various local and national taxes. Thus, the lives of all members of the community were deeply affected by the rabbi and his advisory bodies. The selection of a suitable rabbi was of the greatest importance, for he not only provided personal guidance but also enhanced the status of the community at large.

Gottesman's successor was Tzvi Avigdor Ashkenazi, who held the office from 1814 to 1824. From Galicia, like his predecessor, he brought Munkács to the attention of the Jewish community of Pressburg, which had moved into national prominence thanks to its spiritual leader, Rabbi Moses Sofer (Schreiber), better known by the name Chatam Sofer.[10] Born in Frankfurt-Main, Germany, in 1772, where he received his early training, Chatam Sofer had served a number of other communities before being called to Pressburg in 1806. There he remained until his death in 1839, building up his Yeshivah into the principal center of higher Talmudic studies in Central Europe. His correspondence showed his remarkable erudition and concern for traditional Judaism. His advice and decisions were sought by many rabbis throughout the world. It speaks highly of Tzvi Avigdor Ashkenazi, spiritual leader of the rather small community of Munkács, that several of his inquiries were considered important enough to be answered in detail by the great Rabbi of Pressburg. One deals with the election of a rabbi in a neighboring county—the published reply wisely omits any names—whose candidacy met with local opposition. The candidate claimed the position because his father had occupied it. Tzvi Avigdor Ashkenazy tried to support him, but thought it best to seek the opinion of the Rabbi of Pressburg. Although the inquiry reached the Chatam Sofer while on vacation, he nevertheless proceeded to give a detailed reply. He said that the selection of a candidate must be based on individual merit and approval of the community. He reserved a final decision because he did not know all the facts and "since he would normally be contacted by the civilian authorities for his official judgment."[11] This only indicates how much the Hungarian authorities thought of the Chatam Sofer.

Ashkenazy was followed in 1825 by Rabbi Tzvi Elimelech Spira who stayed in Munkács for only four years, but who made a deep impact by his strict rules and Hasidic orientation. His strength was very much evident in his decisions, to wit: A resident of a neighboring community had deceived the Bet Din by requesting permission to marry a woman who was married already. Rabbi Spira placed the offender in jail and had him brought to a public divorce ceremony in chains. In another case, his published verdict ended, "And if the party does not abide by this decision, the

Bet Din is empowered to approach the civilian authorities to confiscate the offender's property."

Rabbi Spira also organized a society for the education of poor children (*Tamchin De'Orayta*).[12] Membership in this society was based on strict personal behavior, such as wearing of religious garments (*Tzitzit*), praying and daily study. Visits to inns and the playing of cards were prohibited. Talking during prayers in the synagogue also was forbidden. Rabbi Spira even detailed the amount of each individual's financial contributions and the time when these sums should be donated.

Parallel with the strong religious leadership there is also evidence of an increased lay participation in the affairs of the community. This undoubtedly was due to the rise in the number of Jews, which by 1825 amounted to 2,131. After much discussion with the authorities, two community representatives were elected in the same year. Interestingly enough, a layman, Samuel Taub received 27 votes, which was more than given to a rabbi, Yosef Zalman Oestreicher, a student of the Chatam Sofer, who only received 16 votes. In 1829, the authorities passed a new law permitting Jewish ownership of property; this enabled the community to buy land for a new synagogue. The same year saw Rabbi Spira's return to his native Galicia, where he became the spiritual leader of Dynow. One can speculate about the reasons for his departure; perhaps there was local opposition to his strict rules, or maybe Rabbi Spira preferred a smaller geographical responsibility than Bereg County. He died in 1841, widely known in the world of scholarship by the title of his work, *Bene Yisachar*. A few decades later, the name Spira would become identical with religious leadership in Munkács, where his grandson Shlomo, great-grandson Tzvi and great-great-grandson Chaim Elazar followed him in the office of communal rabbi.

The influence of Hasidism must have become very strong during Rabbi Ezriel Gruen's office, which lasted from

1829 to 1841. It led to change of the prayer ritual from the *Ashkenazic* (German) to the *Sephardic* (Spanish) order of service. The former had spread into eastern Europe as the Jews moved from West to East, whereas the latter had become the ritual for Jews living in Mediterranean countries, including Palestine. Sephardic ritual contained many elements of *Kabbala*, which can be described generally as the mystic tradition within Judaism. The teachings and practices of Kabbala had been greatly advanced by Isaac Luria (1534-1572) of Safed in Palestine, where he and his disciples lived a life based on mystic concepts and filled with messianic expectations. Some of their teachings stressed the role of the individual in restoring harmony to a disordered world through intensive prayer and close attachment to God.

The Sephardic ritual, as developed by Luria, appealed to the Hasidic leaders and their faithful followers. It gave them a sense of direction and holiness that permeated all their daily activities. It also afforded them a separate identity and filled them with a greater sense of togetherness. The new spirit was particularly evident in their mode of daily prayer, a practice that has always been part of the observant Jewish man's life style. Let us just read the advice given to the Hasid on how he should perform this hallowed act of praying. It may give us a better understanding of what Hasidism is all about and how it manifests itself to this very day. "A person should pray with deep concentration, heightened ecstasy and complete dedication, prepared to lay down his life for God's name. To create in oneself this sense of holiness, one may even use physical means such as swaying parts of the body, dancing and singing. And just as one should not make light of a drowning man trying to save himself from the water by moving his head and hands, so one should not make light of a person who moves about while praying. For he is only trying to protect himself from evil thoughts that come rushing in on him like treacherous waters bent on disrupting his prayers."[13]

While Hasidism began taking hold of Jewish life in the northeastern parts of the land during the 19th century, important events started to shape Hungary at large, in turn bringing about many changes throughout. There developed a strong drive among the Hungarians for greater political, social and cultural autonomy from the ruling Habsburgs of Austria. This drive culminated in the armed revolt of Hungary under Kossuth in 1848 and 1849, which the Habsburgs managed to suppress with the aid of the Russians. Many Jews, even some from far-away Munkács, actively supported the revolt by joining the armed forces against the Habsburgs.

Undoubtedly, their participation in Hungary's drive for independence was motivated by their yearning to achieve equality before the law. This struggle for equality, often referred to as emancipation, had been one of the burning issues in Jewish life throughout Europe ever since the French Revolution propelled the concept of *"égalité"* (equality) into the minds of all thinking people. In Hungary it became a part of the political reality when, in 1867, the members of Parliament voted to remove all judicial and economic restrictions from their Jewish citizens. This new legislation enabled Jews to play an ever increasing role in Hungary's capitalistic economy. To be sure, the acceptance of equality was never complete. There always remained a strong resentment against Jews on the part of those classes that were dispossessed by the new economy, especially the holders of the large agricultural estates. And while many Jews advanced rapidly in the liberal professions, very few were allowed to serve in public administration. Anti-Semitism remained a strong, ever-ready threat among various clerical and agrarian groups.

The drive for emancipation also affected the internal Jewish stiuation, bringing about new organizational structures, mainly advocated by those living in the cities of central Hungary. They had been the first to adopt the Hungarian language and culture; they had been the first to benefit from the new economic opportunities; and they felt that changes in religious thoughts and practices were a part of the new spirit. They called themselves "Neolog," meaning the advocates of the new doctrines. Fully aware that any changes within the communal structure could not be accomplished without the approval of the Hungarian government, they proposed that a congress be convened to decide on the organization of the Jewish communities. The government accepted the proposal with alacrity in the hope that it would be easier to deal with a unified Jewish community. There was a total of 220 delegates at the Jewish Congress, 126 Neolog and 94 Orthodox, who met in heated discussion from December 14, 1868 until February 23, 1869. Very soon the basic differences between the two groups became evident. The Neolog argued for changes in Jewish education and practice,while the Orthodox insisted that the basis of Jewish life must remain the Jewish laws as laid down in the Shulchan Aruch. When the Neolog majority adopted resolutions that the Orthodox considered a violation of their conscience, a split was inevitable. The Orthodox walked out of the Congress and appealed directly to the Hungarian Parliament for permission to form their own organization. Its being granted reflected the liberal mood of Parliament, which was very sensitive to any issue of religious freedom, a sensitivity sharpened by the constant quarrels between Catholics and Protestants.[14]

Thus, the Congress sparked two autonomous Jewish organizations, one Neolog, whose principal office was in Budapest, and the other Orthodox, whose major center was Pressburg. In some communities they even had a third organization, called "status quo," meaning one that wanted to retain the same position it occupied before the split. The choice of Pressburg for the Orthodox group was only natural in view of the city's religious prominence since the days of the Chatam Sofer. For it had been the principles of Orthodox Judaism, as promulgated by him, that had motivated all the graduates of the Pressburg Yeshivah in their struggle for tradition in all parts of Hungary.

Our own Munkács with its Rabbi Chaim Sofer—no relation to the Chatam Sofer—falls into this category. He had
come to the community as one of the most scholarly spokesmen for Orthodoxy in his time. He had been one of the signers
of the anti-assimilation Mihalowitz declaration of 1866,
which forbade preaching in a language other than Yiddish.
And he had been the one who led the walkout of his Orthodox
colleagues from the Congress in 1869. In this action he represented not only himself, but also his community and the
whole county of Bereg, which by this time had moved completely into the Hasidic fold.[15] But here it must be added that
the Hasidim, while supporting Orthodox autonomy vis-à-vis
the Neolog, had their own stance with respect to Orthodoxy.
This can best be shown by the way Rabbi Sofer fared in his
relations with the community. Although he was respected for
his great scholarship, the Hasidim ultimately parted company with him. For they wanted a *rebbe*, i.e., a learned rabbi
with a "plus." This plus consisted of the rebbe's life style and
the way he interacted with people. They wanted their leader
not to confine himself to his study, but to sit with them at the
table on the Sabbath and Holidays. They wanted to pray, sing
and dance with him in their own way. Thus, ultimately,
Rabbi Sofer left Munkács to become the rabbi of the Orthodox
community of Pest.

The Hasidic character of Munkács also was reflected in
the choice of Sofer's successor. He was none other than Shlomo Spira, grandson fo Tzvi Elimelech, who had been rabbi of
Munkács in the years 1825 to 1829. The new spiritual leader
strengthened the religious life of the people as had his an-
cestor before him and as his son, Tzvi, who followed in 1893,
would do after him. The major problem in the existence of a
religious group revolved around education. The Hungarian
government tried to strengthen its own position by dissemin-
ating its language and culture among the many different
ethnic groups within its borders. This was not easy since
most of them, notably the Ruthenians, Slovaks, Germans,

Croats and Serbs, had languages and cultures of their own. The rabbis, endeavoring to protect the religious traditions of their communities, saw in the government drive a danger. When children had to sit in class without the traditional headcovering, attend school on the Sabbath and engage in secular studies, the outcome soon would be a breaking down of the Jewish way of life, as the rabbis conceived of it. Even though, in due course, the government made allowances for religious observance in their schools or established Jewish schools with Jewish teachers, rabbis like Tzvi Spira were far from being satisfied. They kept exhorting their followers to continue sending their children to the cheder, where their time would be completely devoted to Jewish subjects.

Hindsight tells us that the Hasidim fought an uphill battle, which for the most part, they could not win. First, there was the heavy hand of the government, which penalized those not attending official schools. Jews who only spoke Yiddish were classified as "illiterates." Their Hebrew language training was not recognized at all. Even Rabbi Tzvi himself was denied the title "Communal Rabbi" because of his limited knowledge of Hungarian. Then there were the deplorable physical conditions of the cheder. Frequently the children had to study all day in the same room where the teacher and his family lived. We know that in 1910 the Munkács health authorities, headed by a Jewish doctor, ordered the building of new facilities to protect the health of the children. The teachers of the cheder were very poor because little tuition was paid by poor parents. Yet, a source of conflict within the community lay in the appointment of cheder teachers; Tzvi Spira considered such appointments his own prerogative, but on this he was opposed by other Hasidic groups. Still, the Spira dynasty in Munkács had become strong enough to guarantee that Rabbi Tzvi's son, Chaim Elazar, would follow in his father's position. It was he who would play a dominant role in Subcarpathian Ruthenia after World War I. But before we discuss the changes brought to

Munkács as a result of World War I, we first have to briefly describe the development in other major communities of Subcarpathian Ruthenia.

Ung County and Ungvár

Northwest of Bereg County lay Ung County. Its capital, Ungvár, was approximately 20 miles northwest of Munkács at the foot of the Carpathian mountains.[16] Jewish life already is reported here in the middle of the 17th century, when we hear about the existence of a burial society (*Chevrah Kadisha*). The area belonged to the estate of the Hungarian noble family Drugeth, which after the departure of the Turks at the end of the century, invited immigrants from populous Galicia in the north to settle on their estate. This must have attracted Jewish newcomers, particularly after 1772 when, as we already have heard, Galicia became part of Austria through the partition of Poland. Little is known of the first few rabbis who served the new community, except that they all came from Galicia. The first three were Aryeh Leib Bodek-Reisman, Gedalya Reichseit and Yehuda Fried. The fourth, Tzvi Hirsch Charif-Heller, was succeeded in 1835 by the very learned Meir Eisenstaedter. It speaks well for the community of Ungvár that it was able to attract a rabbi very highly praised by the Chatam Sofer.

Rabbi Eisenstaedter quickly established a Yeshivah with many students who, in turn, provided leadership to many communities throughout Hungary. After the demise of the Chatam Sofer in 1839, Rabbi Eisenstaedter became one of the leading spokesmen for Orthodox Jewry, and his counsel was sought in many quarters. When the Hungarian government approached Jewish leaders for a report on the status of Jewish education, Rabbi Eisenstaedter prepared the reply. He insisted that the situation in the field of education was satisfactory, and there was no need for new textbooks. As for secular education, he said, instruction by non-Jewish teachers was preferable to that of any Jewish teachers who were not respectful of Jewish tradition. He urged the government to establish a commission of eight leading rabbis authorized to ordain new rabbis. Rabbi Eisenstaedter's views, representing the traditional position, were not shared by the liberal elements. But at the time, the Hungarian government did not consider it propitious to inject itself into the internal affairs of the Jewish community. This would come in 1868 when it authorized the convening of the Congress in Budapest. Here one of the key proponents of the Orthodox faction would prove to be Rabbi Eisenstaedter's son, Menachem, who followed in his father's position, serving Ungvár from 1852 to 1870. Despite the younger Eisenstaedter's strong leadership, he was unable to prevent the formation of a Neolog congregation in Ungvár. Too many details are not reported to say very much about this new adventure in independent communal structure. We know the names of the rabbis, Dr. Mór Klein, Ignaz Friedlieber and Martin Deutsch, who served between 1868 and 1906 when this separate organization collapsed, and its members rejoined the regular Orthodox establishment.

A milestone in the educational life of Ungvár was the founding of a Hebrew press in 1864. This was particularly due to Rabbi Shlomo Ganzfried (1804-1886), a native of Ungvár and the grandson of its first rabbi. Ganzfried had received an intensive religious education from early youth, but had never intended to make a living from his rabbinic background. Only after he failed in business did he return to his first love and become in 1850 the head judge of the rabbinic court in Ungvár. In dealing with the many practical issues of Jewish living, he saw the need for a series of publications on the various phases of Jewish law and practice. He wrote a number of guides to religious ritual, which were quickly endorsed by the leading rabbis of his time. But it was his *Kitzur Shulchan Aruch* (Short Guide to Jewish Law) that would establish his name for generations to come. Ganzfried intended to provide the average observant Jew, who had neither the knowledge nor the time to study, with a clearly written book of instructions for every day and all occasions. In this endeavor the author succeeded splendidly as is evidenced by the many editions and translations subsequently published. Interestingly enough, Ganzfried would never allow any commentary by other rabbis to be printed together with his own work. He just did not want to do anything that would confuse the average reader concerned more with *what* he should do than *why* he should do it.[17]

When Menachem Eisenstaedter's son, David, who had followed in his father's position, died after only one year in office (1871), the community of Ungvár was thrown into an election crisis. The elder Eisenstaedter's son-in-law, Rabbi Tzvi Hirsch Weiss, tried to claim the post on the basis of his family ties. Others, however, including leading rabbis of the time, considered Chaim Tzvi Mannheimer from Pistyan a more suitable candidate. Like his predecessors, he was very concerned about the religious life within the community, particularly Jewish education. He served until 1886, much beloved by the many students of the yeshivah, two of whom became well-known in later years. Dr. David Tzvi Hoffmann, a renowned scholar, occupied the post of Rector at the orthodox Hildesheimer Seminary in Berlin, Germany. The other, Dr. Chaim Brody, a native of Ungvár and a grandson of Shlomo Ganzfried, rose to become Chief Rabbi of Prague, Czechoslovakia. He also was known as the foremost scholar of Hebrew poetry in his time.

Mannheimer was followed by Elazar Löw from Ujhely who remained until his death in 1918. He was a remarkable leader who managed to serve a community divided into many divergent groups. The year 1890 saw the establishment of a primary school for boys and girls despite the opposition of the rabbi and the Hasidim. The school was supervised by the government with Hungarian as the language of instruction. The teachers, many of them traditionally oriented educators, were selected by the community, which supplemented their government salaries. Thus, they were accorded a relatively secure economic position. The school drew constant praise from its supervisors and served as a model for similar schools throughout Hungary. Unfortunately, it had only four grades for pupils aged six to ten. Since compulsory education demanded attendance until grade eight, i.e., age 14, all the students had to transfer to other schools. Moreover, the Jewish school only provided education for a tiny fraction of the Jewish children. When the community tried to develop additional facilities, the Hasidim as well as the rabbi opposed it effectively. Their major concern was training in cheder and yeshivah; they were not ready yet for a school that combined religious and secular subjects.

One of Löw's great accomplishments was the construction of a large synagogue that took two years to build (1902-1904). There was much opposition on the part of the local authorities, who objected to its location in the heart of the city, but Löw was strong enough to overcome these obstacles. The order of service was in the Ashkenazic tradition; Löw, however, was wise enough to placate the many Hasidim by helping them to build their own house of prayer and study. These same years, as we already have noted, also saw the dissolution of the Neolog community which was then absorbed by the Orthodox establishment. This too must have been due to Löw's leadership, which tried to maintain unity. During the trying years of World War I (1914-1918), Rabbi Löw rose to the height of his communal concerns when in spite of his advanced age, he cared tirelessly for the many refugees who flooded the city from Galicia. His fine personality was recognized by the Court of Vienna, when Franz Joseph I (1848-1916) conferred upon him the title of Geheimrat (Privy Councillor).

Máramaros County and Sziget

The last of the four northeastern counties to be discussed in detail is Máramaros with its principal city of Sziget, also known as Máramaros-Sziget.[18] As in the other counties, Jewish settlements developed slowly. In 1750, there were only 20 families in Sziget itself. The 1787 census recorded 2,254 persons in the county and indicated a number of small settlements throughout the mountain area. Living conditions were extremely harsh. When the Empress Maria Theresa (1740-1780) raised taxes in 1754, the Jews of Máramaros complained that their only income depended upon the distilling of whisky, which was barely enough for making bread from maize. Moreover, without government protection against their non-Jewish neighbors, as officially promised, they would have to leave. A proverb made the rounds that of the ten measures of poverty in the world, nine went to Máramaros. Rabbi Akiba Yoseph Schlesinger (1838-1922), an early Hungarian champion of Jewish colonization in Palestine, once remarked, "The plan (for settlement in Palestine) was designed to create the modest and quiet village life, whose example I have seen in Hungary, in the villages of Máramaros . . . where the farmer lives from the work of his hands and does not depend on charity."[19] This observation reflects the simplicity of Jewish life in the villages of Máramaros. The hard physical conditions went parallel with limited opportunities for Jewish education. Thus, the people became a relatively easy target for the pseudo-messianic preachings of the aforementioned Jacob Frank who promised them salvation from their misery. From Sziget, Frank's emissaries fanned out to bring his false messages of hope to the isolated mountain villagers. The pseudo-Messiah's conversion to Catholicism in 1759 coincided with reports about a Rabbi Tzvi who had come to Sziget to speak out against the Frankist ideas.

When Rabbi Tzvi died in 1771, no other rabbi is reported for Sziget until more than two decades later. At that time Chaim Traub from Delatyn, Galicia, was elected; his tenure, however, was limited. He first returned to Delatyn in 1800 upon the death of his wife. He remarried, but his second wife died shortly thereafter. Rabbi Traub returned to Sziget and took a third spouse, but passed away in 1802. The void created by this off-and-on rabbinic leadership often was filled by itinerant Hasidic preachers.

We begin hearing about Menachem Mendel (1768-1826) from Kossov, near Kolomea, Galicia, who moved among the Carpathian villages of Máramaros and exhorted the people to joyous Jewish living. He must have had a gift of speaking to persons on their own level, no matter how humble. Menachem Mendel was inspired by the idea of "love of Israel," which encouraged him to travel from village to village and to help its residents in their daily concerns. When he moved his home, in Hasidic terms called "Court," from Kossov to the nearby border town of Vishnitz, Bukovina, it gave his Hasidic followers their name in history. His son Chaim (1795-1844) and his descendants enlarged the role of the Vishnitzer dynasty in the lives of Máramaros and beyond. We shall see that this movement would become of great significance in the world of Hasidism to this very day.

Upon Rabbi Traub's death in 1802, the communal leaders failed to agree on one successor, so they elected two, splitting their rabbinic duties between Sziget and the county. The more important position in the community itself went to Rabbi Yehuda Cohen, whereas Menachem Stern, the other rabbi elected, would devote himself to work in the county. Of Rabbi Cohen little is recorded except that he stayed in office for 17 years and raised a large family, many of whom became rabbis or the spouses of rabbis. As is often the case in history, one hears little of people who did well, but far more about those who did not. This must have been the case with Rabbi Stern, who was criticized as not being fully qualified for his task. To meet some of these challenges, he appointed two assistants for his county duties, a Rabbi Isaac from Borsa and a Rabbi Zundel from Visó. After Rabbi Stern's death in 1834, there was a recurrent conflict as to the choice of a successor. Some opted for Rabbi Stern's son-in-law, a Rabbi

Yoseph Stern, who was a native of Máramaros. The majority, however, led by the prominent Kahane family chose Elazar Nissan Teitelbaum, son of Rabbi Moses Teitelbaum of Ujhely (1759-1841).

Young Teitelbaum marks the arrival on the scene of a family that was destined to play a great role in Hasidism to this very day. The choice of the son undoubtedly was influenced by the high reputation of his father, a native of Przemysl, Galicia, who prior to coming to Hungary had served the Galician community of Szynowa from 1784 to 1808. A great scholar known today as *Yismach Moshe*, (the title of one of his important works), the senior Teitelbaum was held in high esteem by the Chatam Sofer, the foremost religious authority in Hungary. He had embraced Hasidism rather late in life, having been influenced by Rabbi Yaakov Isaac (1745-1815), known as the "Seer of Lublin," one of the outstanding disciples of the Besht himself.

Young Teitelbaum only stayed in Sziget for a few years. By all accounts he was a very retiring person, unable to meet the opposition centered in the person of Yoseph Stern, the earlier contender for the post, who had become one of the judges of the religious court. In this capacity Rabbi Stern appointed a *shochet* (ritual slaughterer), an act that was a direct challenge to the authority of Elazar Nissan Teitelbaum, the communal rabbi. When Rabbi Teitelbaum forbade the shochet to perform his work and he disregarded this order, the battle was on in full. The modern reader must keep in mind that this was more than a question of authority. It was one of great financial impact, since the taxes from the slaughter of animals and the sale of meat were the major source of income for a community. In the case of Sziget, Rabbi Stern and his shochet both belonged to the Vishnitzer Hasidim led by Rabbi Chaim, who supported them to the fullest. This conflict between Hasidic groups is a phenomenon that would appear often in various locations. In our situation in Sziget, Rabbi Teitelbaum lost and left the city in 1840 to be suc-

ceeded by the very Rabbi Stern who had so successfully
defied his authority. But Rabbi Stern too would not enjoy his
newly won positon. He was accused by the head of the Sziget
Yeshivah, Rabbi Yehuda Modern, of making improper ritual
decisions, an accusation that was deplored by other rabbinic
authorities. It was proof of the deep dissension within the
community and bound to do much harm. When Rabbi Stern
died in 1858, the elders must have been very anxious to
restore peace among the various factions, so they elected
Yekutiel Yehuda Teitelbaum (1808-1883), son of the defeated
Elazar Nissan, whose reputation as a fine scholar and a good
speaker had been well established. Undoubtedly, by electing
the son, they tried to make amends for the treatment given the
father. The new Teitelbaum, aware that the major opposition
to his father had come from the Vishnitzer Hasidim, was wise
enough to make a first move towards better relations by
visiting their leader, Menachem Mendel (1830-1885), at his
court in Vishnitz.

The increase in the internal conflicts reflects also the
increase in the Jewish population of Máramaros which grew
from 6,431 in 1825 to 26,295 in 1869. Sziget developed into a
very important political and economic center, but ideologi-
cally its Jews were not close enough to the non-Hasidic
Orthodox leaders of Hungary to participate in the Congress of
1868. They were more under the influence of the Hasidic
leaders of Galicia, whence most of its residents had come. In a
letter Yekutiel Yehuda Teitelbaum wrote,

> We in Sziget have stayed away for ten years from joining the
> (Orthodox) organization of Pest (Hungary) . . . we do not have
> the need for new statutes in our community . . . in this we are
> backed by the great Rebbes of Sanz and Belz (Galicia) . . . truly
> it does not make sense to turn over the reins of communal
> leadership to the residents of Pest, for no matter how great
> their wisdom in their own affairs, they lack insight and un-
> derstanding of Jewish life here in Máramaros.[20]

Nonetheless, a few years later, shortly before his death in

1883, this Rabbi Teitelbaum yielded to the pressure of Hungarian rabbis who urged him to join the autonomous Orthodox body. This move was opposed by a group led by a wealthy member of the community, Kalman Kahane. He left and together with 150 members formed a community of their own. It should be emphasized that this split was one between Hasidic groups and not one of Orthodox versus Neolog. Kahane himself was a deeply religious follower of the famous Hasidic Rabbi Chaim of Sanz (1793-1876). Before leaving he had obtained permission from important Galician rabbis to appoint a shochet for the new community. The reaction of Rabbi Teitelbaum, probably Chananya Yom Tov Lipa (1836-1904), who had succeeded upon his father's death in 1883, was swift and strong. He forbade the eating of meat slaughtered by this shochet. Since Hungarian law did not permit the existence of two communities side by side holding the same name, the Kahane-led community called itself "Sephardic," although all along they claimed to be the original Orthodox group. The depth of the conflict shook the whole rabbinic world at the time. A special court was appointed to arbitrate the issues, but the division could not be bridged. The various charges reflect the dissatisfaction of the minority groups within the Orthodox establishment. And while the major communal power remained with the Teitelbaum dynasty, the Sephardic community continued to function in an increasingly important manner. What originally had been a struggle of one group of Hasidim against another, developed into a more progressive concept of Orthodoxy. In 1906 it led to the election of a university-trained rabbi, Samuel Danzig, who remained in Sziget for 38 years, until the Nazi murderers destroyed him together with his congregation.[21] Dr. Danzig arrived with rich credentials. He was born in 1876 in Vágvecse, Hungary, where his father, Mordechai, served as District Rabbi. Like him, a graduate of the famous Pressburg Yeshivah, young Danzig also studied with Solomon Breuer (1850-1926), the son-in-law and successor of Samson Raphael Hirsch (1808-1888), the fiery leader of Orthodox Jewry at Frankfurt-Main, Germany. He then became a student of philosophy at the universities of Bern, Switzerland, and Munich, Germany, where he obtained his doctorate. Apparently, he was an early adherent to the new movement of Zionism for he attended Zionist Congresses, held in Basel between 1900 and 1905, and reported on their deliberations in the Hungarian press of Budapest. One has to realize that early Zionism had very few religious leaders in its midst: surely it had very few adherents in Hasidic strongholds such as Sziget. Thus the appearance of Samuel Danzig as the spiritual leader of the Sephardic community must have acted like a bombshell. His scholarship and piety, however, soon earned him a place of prominence within the community.

The best proof of Dr. Danzig's high standing was his selection by the Vishnitzer Hasidim to raise funds for the Máramaros *Kolel* in Jerusalem, a community of pious persons who depended upon their fellow Jews for their support. Dr. Danzig forwarded his funds to Israel Hager, the Vishnitzer Rebbe (1860-1936) who transmitted them to Palestine. The Teitelbaum leadership resented this because they saw in it a recognition of Dr. Danzig and his community. In fact, the Vishnitzer Rebbe was urged to forbid the functioning of the Sephardic community's shochet. This the Vishnitzer Rebbe refused for it was his own father, Rabbi Baruch (1845-1893), who had dispatched the shochet. He promised, however, to oppose any Neolog rabbis and their communities. He also agreed to a division of responsibility for the Máramaros Kolel between himself and Rabbi Teitelbaum.

Dr. Danzig's leadership benefited not only his own community, but all of Sziget. He served in the City Council as the leader of the Jewish party and was considered the spokesman for Jewish interests by the Hungarian, and, after World War I, Rumanian governments. Dr. Danzig also became the elo-

quent champion of the new spirit of Zionism, rallying youth
and intellectuals around him. When Dr. Bernard Kahn of the
American Joint Distribution Committee (Joint) visited Sziget
in 1928 for his survey of the welfare needs, it was Danzig who
handed him a memorandum dealing with the history and
social conditions of the Jews of Máramaros.[22]

The story of another personality can further provide us
with an insight into their lives. Hirsch Leib Gottlieb (1829-
1930) was an unusual blend of traditional education, wit and
criticism that enabled him to bring light into the dark corners
of his era. His autobiographical remarks may serve as the best
introduction into his multiple roles as family man, writer,
humorist and critic of his times:

> I was born in the city of Sziget in the year 1829 and educated
> in the Hungarian Yeshivot. As soon as I reached the age of
> eleven, I left my parents' house for the Yeshivah. When I was
> sixteen, I studied in Pressburg under the Ketav Sofer (1814-
> 1872)—[title of Abraham Sofer who had taken over as head of
> the Yeshivah after the death of his father, the Chatam Sofer in
> 1839]. This was the greatest Yeshivah in Hungary. There I
> studied very diligently for I planned to become a rabbi, and I
> would have become one, except for one flaw; my father had
> not been a rabbi. His death forced me to leave the Yeshivah
> and return home. Here I occupied myself with writing Yid-
> dish and Hebrew poetry which made a Badchan[23] (jester) out
> of me. I really became a famous Badchan in all of Hungary,
> Galicia and Rumania. I was asked to perform at all weddings
> of rabbis and rich persons. Subsequently, being a Badchan
> became very unsatisfactory to me and I decided to edit a
> Hebrew newspaper. In 1878[24] a Hebrew paper entitled Ha-
> shemesh (Sun) appeared and due to its excellent articles
> started to shine like the sun. The young people of Sziget
> started to write industriously in Hebrew and I published this
> paper for two years, quietly and satisfactorily . . .. And it came
> to pass at the end of two years' [Genesis XL.1] . . . Suddenly
> the anger of the Sziget Rabbi [Chananya Yom Tov Lipa Teitel-
> baum] erupted. He pretended, that my paper had a bad influ-

ence among the youth, which was becoming irreligious. He
issued a statement, almost like a ban, forbidding the further
reading of *Hashemesh*. This caused the suspension of my
paper and denied me the means of feeding my seven children.
I was forced to leave my home and move to Kolomea, the great
Jewish community in Galicia. Here, I was welcomed with
great honor by the liberal as well as the traditional circles.
They encouraged me to continue publishing *Hashemesh*, but
the laws in Galicia did not permit publication of a weekly
without financial deposit. So I published it one week under
the name *Hashemesh* and the next week under the name
Hachorsa [poetic name for sun], which was a very difficult
undertaking. Fortunately, I had the help of Galicia's best
writers, such as Asher Reuben Broides from Lemberg, Gershom Bader and David Silberbusch from Kolomea. In this
manner I managed to publish the two papers in Kolomea for
three years, but for personal reasons I had to return home to
Sziget. Here I was told by several respected persons that the
rabbi's anger had been caused by my having published in
Hebrew, the Holy Tongue. I was then advised to publish a
paper in Yiddish, to which the rabbi would not object. I
considered this good advice, and soon thereafter my new
paper called *Jewish People's Paper* appeared in the Yiddish
language. Sziget was happy and rejoiced because the new
publication contained news, stories, jokes and songs. In one
word, the whole community, even the Jewish doctors and the
educated classes, who did not care for Yiddish, subscribed to
the *People's Paper*. In time, the idea of Zionism also made
headway in Sziget, and a group was organized with the name
"Love of Zion"; quite naturally, I was one of the founders. A
large meeting took place with many speakers; I too spoke
about Zion, which made a deep impression. This caused the
rabbi to turn against me once more, but this time his ban was
no longer effective. Since the people did not pay any attention
to him, he forbade the publication of the *People's Paper*
altogether. At that time, there existed in Sziget only one
printing press with Hebrew letters, so my paper was forced to
close down. I therefore journeyed to Dr. Herzl, of blessed
memory [he was the founder of Zionism], in Vienna and told

him the whole story. He listened to me sympathetically and asked: 'And now, what do you intend to do?' To which I answered, 'I intend to search for Hebrew lettering in Vienna for the price of a few hundred crowns, and will pay for them in monthly installments.' Dr. Herzl, with a gentle smile, told me to return the following morning at ten. Bidding me farewell, he remarked, 'I will expect you.' The next day I found Dr. Kahan, Dr. Kokosvi and Dr. Herzl in the latter's office and was given 160 crowns for my travel expenses. The office secretary then brought me to the firm of Schwab and Sons, where I placed an order for 800 Crowns. Two months later in Sziget, I received the letters neatly assorted and sufficient for the printing of my paper. Shortly thereafter, the rabbi of Sziget [Chananya Yom Tov Lipa Teitelbaum, died, 1904] of blessed memory, passed away. I then published a paper named *Zion* without any interruption, and also *Love of Zion*, and a monthly called *The Truth*, up to the outbreak of World War I.

Yes, in this manner I sacrificed my best years for literature and culture in the dark corners of Máramaros.[25]

Gottlieb died at the age of 101, poor and disappointed that his work had met with such opposition. He deserves a place of honor in this volume for all his efforts in behalf of the Hebrew language and an enlightened public. He most certainly was far ahead of his time.[26]

By concentrating on Ungvár, Munkács and Sziget, we must not forget that there were many other communities in Subcarpathian Ruthenia, which perhaps were not as large in numbers, but nevertheless had important personalities and were rich in accomplishments. One was Rabbi Moses Schick of Huszt, who served in this city from 1861 to 1879. He was a great scholar and developed his yeshivah into a widely recognized center of study, which attracted students from all parts of Hungary. Although not a Hasid himself, he felt very comfortable in Huszt with its strong Hasidic atmosphere. The same may be said of one of his successors, Moshe Grünwald, who headed the community from 1893 to 1920. Another place to recall here is Spinka, which became a center of Hasidism and gave its name to a Hasidic group still active to this very day. Two of their leaders stand out prominently, Yoseph Meir Weiss (1839-1909) and his son, Yizchak Eisik (1875-1944). Then there was the city of Szöllös with its Rabbi Shmuel Shmelke Klein (1805-1875), a great and saintly scholar. As a strict traditionalist he was very much opposed to those who wanted to take time for secular studies. When told that some parents wanted their children to learn French, he remarked in jest, "What is so special about French? In France, any child of the simplest peasant knows it." Briefly mentioned as centers of Hasidism also should be the small town of Kaszony with its rabbis from the Rottenberg family and the Transylvanian community of Dés with its rabbis from the Paneth family.[27]

While all of these communities perished in the Holocaust, the activities of one of the more recent Hasidic rabbis continue to this very day in Israel. Aaron Roth, also known as Reb Arele, was born in Ungvár in 1894. He attracted a following almost against his will and only upon the urging of his Hasidic teachers. Not being a descendant of a Hasidic dynasty, his personality and his teachings alone made him attractive to small groups in Hungary and later in Palestine, where he found refuge prior to World War II. Gershom Scholem, the great interpreter of Hasidic thought, has placed him into the exalted category of the early founders of the Hasidic movement. After Reb Arele's death his followers split into two groups, one led by his son-in-law and the other by his son. Reb Arele emphasized the need for simple faith, rejecting any compromises with modern views. He looked upon suffering as a punishment for abandoning faith and constantly called for repentance. It may be best to end this chapter by quoting him directly:

> I believe with perfect faith that no accidents happen which are not intended by God Almighty. Furthermore, I believe that there is no creature above or below that can do good or

harm, or act in anything, even the slightest movement, without power coming from Him, be He blessed, for all is provided by the Owner of the will, the Leader who leads His world with kindness and mercy.[28]

And finally, he wrote in a letter, "My dear child, the main thing is that one should be God's soldier and serve Him day and night . . . and struggle with animal desires . . . and make one's speech gleam with integrity and faith . . ."

2. WORLD WAR I TO WORLD WAR II (1914–1939)

The outbreak of World War I in August, 1914, brought an end to the peaceful development of Hungary and all its counties. Hungary, a part of the Central Powers, had to gather its forces to stem the onslaught of the Russians in the East. Many men were called up to serve, disrupting families and communities; approximately 10,000 Jewish soldiers were killed.[1] The Russian armies, which had swept into Galicia by late August, caused a great number of Jews to cross the Carpathian mountains into Hungary, where they hoped to escape the ravages of the battle zones. Russian troops also reached the northeastern Hungarian counties, which forced many families to flee into the interior of Hungary, Austria and Germany. Ungvár, Munkács and Sziget became swollen with refugees, straining the resources of these cities. Another influx took place in 1916 when Jewish families tried to escape the invading Rumanian troops that broke into the southern part of Transylvania. The miseries of war increased even further when the Austro-Hungarian empire collapsed in November, 1918. In its wake many changes were wrought within the four counties, now better described as Subcarpathian Ruthenia.[2] At first, there were intense political negotiations as to which state should take over this area. The major issue was the Ruthenians who amounted to approximately 450,000 out of a total population of approximately 725,000. To quote the historian Magocsi: "Throughout their history they had

29

been equally influenced by, and in turn had influenced, neighboring Galician-Ukrainian, Slovak, and Magyar cultures.[3] Thus, at the time of decision as to which country Subcarpathian Ruthenia should be attached to, there were theoretically several choices. Ultimately, the views of the victorious Allies prevailed (coupled with the liberal approach of the new Czechoslovak leaders), and Subcarpathian Ruthenia became a part of Czechoslovakia with the understanding that they would become an autonomous unit.

The Jewish situation also was beset with difficulties, although of a somewhat different nature. They only constituted about 12 per cent of the population, totaling approximately 90,000 people. All through the years they had never constituted themselves as a national minority. Many had accepted integration into Hungarian society as a desirable program; indeed, they had often become the leaders of Hungarian culture. This was a direct result of the spirit of liberalism and economic opportunity prevailing in Hungary until World War I. The economist Végházi describes the period as follows:

> The Jews who, with a few exceptions, a short while before had only spoken German, now mastered the Hungarian language with amazing speed. They became acquainted with Hungarian culture which they helped to develop further, and found ways to introduce into Hungary the results of economic developments achieved abroad . . . Jews not only became an important factor in the economic life of Hungary, but also sought ways and means to become significant in politics and in the artistic and scientific life of the country. As their influence increased, they felt more and more in harmony with the country, and considered themselves to be Hungarians who practised the Jewish religion.[4]

All this, of course, involved a high degree of assimilation, often resulting in conversion, a danger that had been foreseen by the religious leaders in all parts of the country, particularly the Hasidic areas of the northeast. The struggle of the rabbis was difficult because they were facing a formidable trend. Although this area had little industry and was principally agricultural, everybody benefited from the economic advance of the country as a whole. Ungvár, Munkács and Sziget became commercial centers of Subcarpathian Ruthenia, with the Jewish share of its population as high as 43 per cent. All had to abide by government policy, which required from everyone a basic knowledge of Hungarian. While the rabbis tried to maintain their own cheder-Talmud-Torah-yeshivah school system, they were forced to make provisions for the basic knowledge of Hungarian and secular subjects. One of the means of combating the trend of secularization was the cultivation of the Yiddish language for daily use and study. Yiddish was more than a language, it was part of one's religion and tradition. It was the language of those who fought assimilation and tried to maintain the religious way of life.[5] Of course, the choice was not either/or even among the most Orthodox Rabbis of the region. There were various degrees of acceptance of Hungarian language and government, even in very Hasidic circles. The best example is Rabbi Chaim Elazar Spira of Munkács whom we have already met. He would dominate the scene until his demise in 1937, becoming one of the three members of a league for the protection of Hungary's political integrity. The league was formed at the end of World War I when the question of Hungary's minorities was on the agenda of the Allies. This ultimately led to the Treaty of Trianon in 1920, making Subcarpathian Ruthenia a part of Czechoslovakia, with one important exception involving Máramaros county and its large city of Sziget. To quote Magocsi:

> Originally Rumania expected Russia to annex Subcarpathian Rus. In the secret treaty signed with the Allies in 1916, the Tisa River was set as the future boundary between the two states. When Russia was no longer a contender for the territory, Prime Minister Bratianu claimed for Rumania all of Máramaros County, so as to extend its common frontier with Po-

lish-occupied Galicia. But the Council of Foreign Ministers at the Peace Conference rejected his request, and the Rumanians only received those parts of Máramaros county south of the Tisa.[6]

The principal objective motivating the Ruthenian leaders in the direction of Czechoslovakia was their hope of becoming autonomous. This hope, however, did not materialize for many reasons, among them that the people were not ready for it. There were too many crosscurrents and internal factions, which made autonomy difficult, even if the Czech government had really wanted to see it accomplished. Similarly, the Jews, who did not have nationality status under the Hungarians, were not prepared for such a development under the Czechs, certainly not in the beginning. Yet, just as the active support of those Ruthenians who had immigrated to the United States around the turn of the 20th century helped their kin in the old country, so were Jews in the United States instrumental in helping their brethren towards nationality status and minority rights. Immediately after the war, the Jews of Subcarpathian Ruthenia were mainly concerned with binding up their wounds, finding food and clothing for their families and medical attention for their sick.

The fighting in this region had lasted deep into 1919. In the city of Munkács, for example, after the end of Austro-Hungarian rule in late October 1918, there was first the short-lived Hungarian republic under Count Mihály Károlyi and then the Soviet-Hungarian republic under Béla Kun. To meet these forces, Czech legionnaires were ordered to advance towards Ungvár to the west and Beregszász to the south. The community organized a civilian guard from the ranks of Jewish soldiers just returned from service in the Hungarian army. In February 1919, the Ukrainian Cossack bands under Petlura attempted to take over Munkács together with other Ruthenian territory, which they claimed on the basis of common language and race. Their reputation as killers and plunderers brought great fear into the Jews of Munkács. But with the active support of Chaim Elazar Spira, the communal rabbi, the Jewish guard met this crisis successfully. They waited for the bands at the train station, disarmed them and chased them back to Galicia. In the words of Rabbi Isaac Klein, an eyewitness, "The Pogromchicks were basically cowards and struck only when there was no resistance."[7] Angry over their failure in Munkács, the bands attacked the Jews of Proskurov, Galicia, in March 1919, killing many men, women and children.[8] Shortly after the encounter with the Cossacks, Rumanian troops entered Munkács from the south and Czech troops from the west. Finally, the Rumanians moved out and the Czech administration took over the city and territory. All these military and political upheavals came to a formal end with the Treaty of Trianon of 1920, which made Subcarpathian Ruthenia a part of Czechoslovakia.

American Joint Distribution Committee's Aid

Ever since the beginning of the war, Jewish relief efforts had been organized through the American Jewish Joint Distribution Committee (universally known as "Joint"), providing aid to Jews wherever needed.[9] Its members, under the leadership of Felix M. Warburg, were anxiously watching the scene in Central Europe, particularly in Eastern Galicia, Eastern Poland and the Ukraine, where hundreds of thousands had died as a result of epidemics and pogroms. The Jews were victims of the war between Bolsheviks and their anti-Semitic White Russian opponents. We have already learned that Petlura and his hordes had even penetrated south of the Carpathian mountains. The fighting in this region made it impossible for any Joint representative in 1919 to come directly to the aid of Subcarpathian Ruthenia, even though on March 22, 1919, Henry G. Alsberg had already set up in Prague a relief committee for Jews in Czechoslovakia. It was soon realized that the major area of need was in the eastern province of Czechoslovakia, where approximately 100,000 men, women and children lived, joined by thousands of refugees from

Galicia, Poland and Russia. At first, the war economy under Hungary, then the changed political boundaries plus the lack of transportation facilities, made it most difficult for these people to secure food, clothing and medical supplies. The kitchens set up by the American Relief Administration (ARA)[10] were not patronized by the local Jews because their food was not kosher; little could be done with money because the supplies needed could not be purchased locally. In order to fully investigate conditions, Leon Wechsler and Hetty Goldman visited Ungvár (now called Uzhorod by the Czechs), on June 28, 29 and 30, 1920, and Munkács (now called Mukacevo) on July 1.

In response to the appalling conditions, it was decided to establish the Joint headquarters in Munkács which was geographically more central than Ungvár, the capital, and thus better located for dispatching supplies to the needy villages. Moreover, ARA and the Czech Red Cross also operated in this city, making for better coordination of all relief activities. It was further decided to immediately telegraph Alexander Landesco, another Joint representative who visited Rumania to purchase two carloads of flour for shipment to Munkács.[11] The ARA representative, Thomas Temple, offered his warehouse for storage of any food sent into the country. He also reserved 3,000 portions of food for Jewish children and opened up special kosher kitchens wherever necessary. Milk and fats were shipped in from Holland and clothing from the Czech provinces with the help of the Red Cross. With transportation a major problem, cooperation of the local Government authorities was most important and fortunately speedily forthcoming through Subcarpathian Ruthenia's Governor Gregory I. Zsatkovich, an American lawyer of Ruthenian heritage who had been very active in American-Ruthenian affairs and came to Czechoslovakia to continue this work. The Governor promised to help and to give these relief efforts the widest publicity.[12] The Joint, looking to staff its Munkács office, also found an American in the person of Dr. M. Olkon, a Chicago physician, who began working July 19, 1920. He made a trip by foot and wagon through the mountain villages and in August reported the pitiful conditions. He said there was gradual starvation, people virtually going naked and little employment. Tuberculosis, typhus and dysentery were rampant in the refugee-filled villages. Olkon urged the establishment of a Jewish hospital to serve the population, as they were averse to being treated in a non-Jewish facility. A similar request is recorded a year later in Pressburg (now called Bratislava), where the Orthodox community urged the founding of a Jewish hospital for Slovakia and Subcarpathian Ruthenia, since the only other Jewish hospitals were in Vienna and Budapest. Dr. Emanuel Fraenkel succeeded Dr. Olkon who had only remained three months. He organized his work together with the local Czech authorities and the Jewish community of Munkács, complaining in his report to the Joint of an unsuccessful attempt to obtain the cooperation of the few rich local Jews: " . . . they prefer to attend to their own affairs and to leave the social care to others." He tried to improve the medical situation by furnishing existing clinics with free medical supplies for the poor and making arrangements with the few local doctors for similar treatment of the needy. The lack of bathhouses and soap contributed to the poor sanitary conditions, causing the spread of infectious diseases. His report includes the following horrible statistics: "This section has 3,300 widows, 900 as a result of the war, 2,000 whose husbands died of sickness and 400 where husbands are missing for the past two years. There are 6,800 orphans of which 5,000 are fatherless, 1,000 full orphans and 800 war orphans."

The work of the Joint stimulated regional cooperation and organization among people not greatly accustomed to it. By establishing a total of 150 local committees with a central office in Munkács, they were able to stir up dormant forces within the community, leading to greater self-help. These committees also put the people in a better position for presenting their demands to the government authorities. Thus, we learn, in 1922 the government intended to establish sewage systems and proper water supplies in the four major cities: Ungvár, Munkács, Szöllös and Beregszász (now Beregovo).

Closely connected with the improvement of health conditions was the question of economic recovery. In order to understand the role played by the Joint we should first read from a contemporary's report on conditions that remained basically unchanged throughout the 1920's:

> Two-thirds of the population, about 65,000, lived in rural and mountainous areas and only one-third in the towns. The economic situation of the rural Jews was not substantially different from that of the Ruthenian peasants, who made up the bulk of the population. The main income was from agriculture, and like their non-Jewish neighbors, there were those among them who benefited from the introduction of more efficient methods of farming. In most of the villages, however, where primitive methods remained in use, harvests and profits continued to be meager.

> The main agricultural pursuits of the Jewish rural population was sheepherding, fruit-growing and honeymaking. Many Jews worked in the lumber industry not only as merchants, but also as woodcutters, mill hands and raftsmen. Others were employed as carriers, either as day laborers or independent wagoners. Jews were also active in such trades as shoemaking, tailoring, iron-and-tin-smithers, and the like. Occasionally one came across rural Jewish 'gentry,' i.e. owners of farmland, timberland and salt quarries.[13]

Ever since the Joint had opened its office in Munkács in July of 1920, it engaged in fact finding, which finally culminated in a statistical report on the professional distribution of the Jewish population. It is quoted in full:

PROFESSION	FAMILIES	INDIVIDUALS
Agricultural workers, shepherds	2,500	12,500
Village laborers, unskilled workers	2,000	10,000
Wagoners	1,200	6,000
Skilled workers (tailors, shoe-makers, carpenters, tinsmiths)	1,380	6,900
Tavern keepers	1,180	5,900
Shop owners	1,500	7,500
Businessmen	900	1,500
Professionals (doctors, lawyers, engineers)	200	800
Butchers	100	400
Manufacturers	100	400
Teachers (private Hebrew teachers)	800	4,000
	11,860	55,900[14]

This survey accounts for approximately 60 per cent of the population. The remaining 40 per cent had no definable source of income and must be put in the unemployed or unproductive column. Another unanswered question is how much income the various groups derived from their given professions. In 1921 there was no way of arriving at such sophisticated statistics. The whole region, which had oriented itself commercially toward Budapest and Vienna until World War I, had to find new contacts leading to Prague, the capital of Czechoslovakia. It was always Joint policy to try to develop the local resources in any given area and thereby help the people to stand on their own feet. This was clearly expressed in the large conference of leading members of all communities which was held in Munkács in August, 1922. The Joint representative, Dr. Emanuel Fraenkel, reviewed the activities, which started out as direct relief, then care of orphans and improvement of health conditions. Now the most important task was economic reconstruction. He called for self-help which would unite all the various factions within the communities. There were some who had given up hope for the Jews living in the mountains. Here, he said, we have a good group, eager to work, traditional and bound to the earth, but cut off from the intelligentsia of the city. They are the real martyrs because they are on a lower cultural, economic and intellectual platform. He moved away from the concept of handouts, calling for greater productivity and a giant move toward industrialization. This would include turning water-power into electricity and exploitation of the huge lumber resources. It would be done through establishment of trade schools for the younger generation and long-term, low-interest loans for the older generation.

The deliberations led to improvements in some areas. By 1923, 14 Jewish savings and loan societies began functioning. Between 1924 and 1930 they received more than five million dollars in low interest loans from the Joint, which enabled them to expand their activities as follows:

	NUMBER OF MEMBERS	AMOUNT LENT
1924	2,580	$11,600,000
1925	2,294	8,500,000
1926	3,696	10,300,000
1927	4,683	13,000,000
1928	5,415	13,000,000
1929	7,210	17,000,000
1930	9,830	22,900,000

In this drive for economic recovery a fine example of cooperative spirit should be recorded. In Trnovo and Teresvon, one of the poorest areas of the province, the Jews sought to create new economic opportunities through the construction of a railroad. When the authorities refused to budget funds for the project, they decided to build it anyway. Every Jew between the age of 18 and 60 volunteered three days of labor, or two days and a wagon with draft animals. Land-owners contributed the lumber free of charge.

The reconstruction conference of 1922 held in Munkács provides another insight into Jewish life. It shows the individual party affiliation of each participant. Among the 28 present, nine were Orthodox, five Zionist, four Assimilationist, two Democratic, two Social-Democrat, one Radical-Socialist and five were marked as "without a party." This may sound a bit confusing and requires an explanation. "Orthodox" meant that one belonged to the Orthodox community, which represented the religious outlook of the individual. Zionist and Assimilationist reflected groupings within the community. The other affiliations represented existing Czech parties for which the individual voted. These local groupings covered a wide variety of opinions. How about the national scene? The picture is equally bewildering and difficult for the modern reader to follow.

Minority Status

With the establishment of the new state of Czechoslovakia in 1919, the Jews had been granted official recognition as a national minority.[15] One benefit of the new status was representation in the legislative bodies of the state. A great step forward, this was hailed by most as a guarantee for individual rights in every area of local and national activity. A National Jewish Council was organized to promote a newly formed Jewish party, which would have its own representatives in the Parliament in Prague. The law stipulated that 20,000 votes were needed to elect a representative. In the first election of 1920, the Jewish party received 80,000 votes, which should have given them four representatives. But, due to irregular distribution of its votes, it did not receive any representative at all. The Jews of Subcarpathian Ruthenia had not participated in this election; they had been busy binding up their war wounds and getting on their feet economically. The average person, moreover, had to adjust to the new

concept of individual rights and his sudden ability to influence Government decisions through votes. While the new
constitution may have promulgated certain provisions to
protect the Jews and other national minorities, particularly
the large number of Ruthenians, the Czech officials executing
these provisions often were very slow in doing so. We already
have seen that in Subcarpathian Ruthenia approximately 65
per cent were Ruthenian, 12 per cent Jewish and 15 per cent
Hungarian. Under the Hungarian administration before
World War I, the Jews had been put into the Hungarian
column whenver a census was taken. Under the new regime
the Czech officials were not interested in strengthening the
minorities at the expense of the national administration.

An office for the defense of Jewish rights was opened by
the Jewish party in Ungvár in 1921, in an unsuccessful effort
to secure better results in the 1924 election. There was no
question that the sympathies of many Jewish voters lay with
the Jewish party. Even Rabbi Chaim Elazar Spira, the Hasidic
leader of Munkács, had identified himself with the Jewish
party with the proviso, "opposed to Zionism." Like many of
his contemporaries, he saw the drive for a Jewish homeland
as a movement led by secular leaders, denying traditional
concepts of Judaism and undermining the sacred beliefs of
his followers. Since the Jewish party was Zionist-oriented, he
felt that his interests would be better served by the Agrarian
party. These interests included the setting up of a central
"bureau" which would coordinate all Orthodox religious
congregations in Subcarpathian Ruthenia locally and not
come under the jurisdiction of the Bratislava (Pressburg)
bureau. Rabbi Spira distrusted some of the Orthodox rabbis of
Slovakia, whom he already considered too modern in outlook. For similar reasons, this fiery leader refrained from
supporting Agudath Israel of Slovakia, whose opposition to
secular Zionism did not seem ardent enough to his thinking.[16] The Agrarian party, interested in obtaining the votes of
Rabbi Spira and his followers, promised him their support.

Thus, again in 1924, there was no Jewish delegate sent to the National Parliament in Prague. The Jewish party did not even obtain 20,000 votes, which was particularly sad because the Senate candidate had been Professor Chaim Brody, Chief Rabbi of Prague and a native of Ungvár.

In his desire to control congregational activities, Rabbi Spira also battled a famous Hasidic leader, Rabbi Isachar Dov Rokeach of Belz, Galicia, who had sought refuge in Munkács, where he had a large following during World War I.[17] The city had become a center of many Hasidic rabbis, all trying to find shelter there. The conflict between Spira and Rokeach was full of mutual recriminations. Ultimately, Spira induced the authorities to withdraw permission for the rabbi from Belz to remain, forcing him to leave in 1923. This only increased the opposition of the Belzer Hasidim against the authority of Rabbi Spira.

Education

Another area greatly influenced by the Czech government's policy of minority rights was education. It involved every Jewish family that had children of school age. The choice of a school, never easy, had always depended greatly upon the types available and the attitude of the individual parents. But now there was the question: "What is the official language of Subcarpathian Ruthenia?" More specifically, what was the language of the Ruthenians who represented 65 per cent of the population? Was it Russian, Little Russian (Ukrainian) or a particular dialect?[18] Under the Hungarian government there had been no dispute on the official language, even in areas where the bulk of the people spoke a different language at home. With compulsory education a matter of law, the official tongue had been Hungarian and over the years everyone had become familiar with it. Now, under the Czechs the area was supposed to become autonomous and a whole variety of schools with special languages developed: Hungarian for the local intelligentsia and Ruthenian for the native population. Then there were Czech schools spreading the language of the Prague government which mainly was spoken by officials and their families. Finally, came schooling in German, spoken by only about 2 per cent of the population, but often used in Jewish circles as a "language of contact." As one report describes it: a language used by fellow Jews in and outside Czechoslovakia.

The confused political situation following World War I impaired the educational opportunities for Jewish children; in spite of their new minority status. Actually, things had worsened since the Hungarian schools, which most Jewish children had attended in the past, no longer represented the official language. The freshly organized schools with the Czech tongue were really too new for the Jews to feel comfortable in them. Moreover, those who did attend were accused by the Hungarians of being traitors to their mother tongue. On the other hand, the Ruthenian schools were not favored by Jewish parents because their general standards were lower than desirable and they preached Ruthenian culture. Sole, himself a teacher during this period, made this observation which is worth quoting for its color and insight:

> The comical as well as the tragic side of this (Jewish children attending Ruthenian schools) came to light when, for instance, such a child brought home a gift at the end of the school year with the inscription, "because of his progress and excellent behavior," the gift being a picture of Alexander Dochanovic, the Ruthenian poet, priest and author of the Carpatho-Ruthenian hymn. The child anticipated a warm and festive reception at home for the gift, but instead, his angry father took hold of him and his picture and threw both of them out, saying, "What else . . . he will hang up a priest for us on the wall next . . ."

And another example: A Jewish child had to memorize a famous Ruthenian song, the content of which was, "I was a Ruthenian, and I am and always shall be, for I was born to a Ruthenian mother and father." Naturally, the parents who understood Ruthenian could not swallow these words calmly, and they did not let the child continue his memorizing.

Hebrew National Movement

One group in Munkács, in particular, must have been very unhappy over this lack of Jewish identity in the government-financed schools, be they Ruthenian, Czech or Hungarian. This was the group that had begun thinking about Zionism, the Hebrew language and Jewish statehood. Organized Zionist activities were slow in coming to this city. A first group had been formed in 1912, but the rabbi at that time, Rabbi Tzvi Spira, called all the young members individually and forbade them to join. After the war and the return of the soldiers, who had seen and heard much about the national movement, a new group formed. This group organized circles, which then led to the founding of a Hebrew-speaking school in 1920/21. Many obstacles had to be overcome in the first year when the enrollment amounted to 45. Teachers, textbooks, facilities and funds had to be obtained. The government had made no provisions in its budget for such a project, although theoretically it was very much in line with the new concept of nationality and minority rights. Then there was Rabbi Spira, who forbade attendance at a school based on Zionist ideas. Still in spite of all odds, the school of Munkács was soon followed by others in major communities. In 1923, they formed a network of nine schools with 950 students, which were supervised by the government authorities in Ungvár. While this recognition was a tremendous achievement, the schools could depend on government support for merely 10 per cent of their budgets. The rest had to come from monthly contributions of parents and friends throughout the province. The Joint and its cultural committee, headed by Dr. Cyrus Adler, also was involved in financial assistance to the Hebrew school program, which was widely acclaimed for its results. In 1923, it even drew praise from a representative of the League of Nations, who came to observe the schools. Of course, the Czech government was interested in showing the world that its minorities were well treated. It also expected that its support of the Hebrew school program would attract Jewish voters in the forthcoming elections of 1924.

A logical sequence to the establishment of the Hebrew elementary school was, of course, the creation of a Hebrew high school. What may have been simple logic, however, was more difficult to execute for a major problem arose in finding the proper individual to organize this project. He eventually was found in the person of Dr. Chaim Kugel; and the story of the Hebrew high school, or as it was known, the Hebrew Gymnasium is very much the story of this man. It is a fascinating one, which should not be forgotten.[19]

Kugel was born in 1897 in Minsk, White Russia, and had been a student in Palestine until shortly before the outbreak of World War I, when he had returned to Minsk to visit his parents. The war prevented him from resuming his studies in Palestine, and he continued them in Poland, ending up in Prague, Czechoslovakia, in 1920. All throughout his student years and particularly in Prague, he had been active as a teacher of Hebrew and leader of Zionist activities. He was widely known for his dedication to Zionist ideals. Thus, when the search for the Munkács program began, he seemed to be the ideal choice. In 1924, however, there was only an idea, but no definite plans as to the school's curriculum, facilities, funds or teachers. Kugel himself was really a stranger to the community, not even a Czech citizen, when he first arrived in Munkács. Nevertheless, he soon impressed everyone with his zeal and energy.

First, he had to battle with the Czech authorities who refused to grant a permit. To make Hebrew the language of education for a Gymnasium—instructing students in all subjects and qualifying them for further studies in universities—was unheard of in Czech educational circles. Then there were the objections of the assimilationist Jews, who saw in the

revival of nationalist ideals a threat to their own status in
Czech society. But the strongest opposition came from Rabbi
Spira and his followers, who viewed the Gymnasium as a
threat to the traditional Jewish way of life. In spite of all the
difficulties, Kugel persisted in his efforts, which were ultimately crowned with success. Not only did the school attract
students who became ardent spokesmen for Hebrew language and Zionist ideas, but it also gained a large number of
friends throughout the country and the Jewish world. In the
United States, a request for support, addressed to Dr. Cyrus
Adler of the Joint's cultural committee in 1927, pointed out
that only 40 percent of the school's budget could be met from
local sources, a problem which reflected the general poverty
of the region. [20] The financial basis of the school was
strengthened in 1929, when the Jewish party, allied with the
Polish one, managed to obtain two seats in the Parliament.
This enabled the Jewish representatives to make financial aid
a national issue. By 1932, when the school, with well-
deserved pride and ceremony, celebrated its first graduation,
the number of students had risen to 232. Even if one adds to
this number the approximately 1,000 pupils attending the
Hebrew public schools, it still must be considered rather
small, particularly when comparing it to the 13,000 Jewish
children attending public school in Subcarpathian Ruthenia
in 1924. Nevertheless, it represents a great achievement in
view of all the obstacles that had to be overcome.

The school was more than just a place to educate a few. It
served as a center of national Jewish spirit for the whole
province and country. This is very much evident from the
illustrated jubilee volume, published in honor of its first
graduating class in 1932.[21] Leading representatives of the
country expressed their pleasure over this occasion, including Dr. Ivan Derer, Minister of Education, Dr. Anton Beskid,
Governor of Subcarpathian Ruthenia and numerous Jewish
leaders of prominence. Beskid's statement is quoted in full
for its special understanding of Jewish needs. At the same

time, it expresses his hope that improved Jewish conditions would aid the cause of Ruthenian autonomy:

> I welcome with joy the opening of the Hebrew Gymnasium in Munkács. I regarded this initiative as one of the ways of improving the position of the Jews of Subcarpathian Ruthenia. This position was hardly favorable. In the past, I had occasion to point out that the impoverished Jewish masses were unprepared to face the rebirth of the Ruthenian people.
>
> With deep satisfaction I noticed that the leaders of the Jewish people at the time realized that through my observations I attempted to help the Jews in their undeserved troubles. Again, I became convinced of the blessed spirit which prevailed in the Hebrew Gymnasium of Munkács. During my visit in 1929, I myself saw the high standard of education and discipline of the Gymnasium, its favorable views about the State and the other people living in Subcarpathian Ruthenia. I wish the Hebrew Gymnasium the best success in its endeavors, so necessary for its prosperity.[22]

Jewish-Ruthenian Relations

Beskid's understanding attitude is also evidenced by his involvement in the conflict between the bureau of Orthodox communities and the Zionist leadership of the province. Behind the bureau stood Rabbi Spira, who wanted to be independent of the Pressburg office. This dream of independence could not be realized without the moral and financial support of the authorities. As already noted, the rabbi worried that control of the communities would be unduly influenced by the Zionists, thereby undermining his authority to demand strict compliance with Jewish laws. The Zionists, though numerically weak, were very strong in their desire to develop a new spirit within the community. To that end they established the Hebrew school system which grew rapidly in spite of Rabbi Spira's violent opposition. The Zionists also became very active in social and welfare matters, increasing their influence considerably. Upon seeing the success of the

Zionists, the Orthodox also tried to involve themselves in social matters. Dr. Beskid attempted to bring the two parties together in hopes of discovering a common ground for the benefit of social programs affecting the whole community. At first, the Orthodox refused to sit down at a round-table conference with the Zionists, particularly under the chairmanship of the non-Jewish governor; they were afraid that Beskid would side with the Zionists. Aside from the basic differences between the parties, there also was the question of which language to use in negotiating. Hungarian, which all spoke very well, was not acceptable since it was not the official language of the country, whereas Czech, the official medium, was not mastered by all participants. Thus, it was decided to negotiate in Yiddish which was also understood by Beskid. This solution reflects favorably upon Beskid, who could have asked that the language be Ruthenian (also understood by all).

It also illustrates the close relations that existed between Jews and Ruthenians, particularly in the 1920's. Both groups had been neglected in the past and both were trying to improve their lot; the Ruthenians strove toward autonomy, and the Jews toward implementation of their minority rights. The new Czech officials, failing to understand either of them, were slow in advancing their causes. The close relations between Ruthenians and Jews were based on mutual needs. The peasants brought their produce to the market and the Jews did the trading for them. To quote Sole:

> They spoke a common language, Ruthenian. In his heart the peasant knew that the average Jew was no better off than himself, and had to struggle equally hard to earn his bread and educate his children. The daily lives of the two groups were very similar, and many Ruthenian peasants were well-acquainted with Jewish ways and customs, which they were careful to respect. They were glad to perform chores for the Jew on the Sabbath, especially in return for a piece of Jewish Halla, Gefillte fish, or some other delicacy. In the towns many

non-Jewish girls worked as domestics in Jewish homes, cleaning, cooking and taking care of the children. Such women became "experts" in Jewish life, and would watch over the children in their care with an eagle eye lest they commit the slightest ritual infraction. They instructed the children to say their morning prayers in Hebrew and understood Yiddish very well.

Whereas Jewish and Ruthenian adults mingled daily in businesses and offices, their children mixed even more freely in the schools, streets, athletic fields, etc. On occasion an anti-Semitic remark might lead to blows, but the Jewish boys were quick to defend themselves, and there was little incentive to pick on them. (After 1938, of course, this situation changed drastically.)

Thus, we see that in the daily round of life, Jewish and non-Jewish youngsters were active together in practically every area. In addition, there were individual Jewish organizations; this was especially true in the field of sports, where Jewish boys excelled. With the exception of the most assimilated circles, friendships were uncommon between Jewish girls and Gentile boys, and even rarer between Gentile girls and Jewish boys.

For all that the two groups shared in common, the line of demarcation between Jew and Gentile remained clear, particularly in the big towns where the Jewish population was large and self-sufficient in most of its needs.[23]

The capital city of Ungvár, with a total population of 40,000, affords a fine illustration of the cordial treatment as extended to its approximately 12,000 Jews. Traffic came to a halt and business life quieted down on the Sabbath. Jews were prominent in city and municipal Government. A Jewish doctor headed the municipal hospital; of 45 elected city councilors, 17 were Jews elected on various lists, including one of the Jewish Party. The street in front of the Hebrew Elementary School was named after Dr. Theodor Herzl; another bore the name of Dr. Benjamin London, a well-known physician and honorary citizen.[24]

There was a marked difference between Ungvár and Munkács, which was only about 30 miles further to the East. Life was quieter and more orderly in Ungvár; this was probably due to the fact that Ungvár was more of an administrative center, whereas Munkács was the major commercial city of the province. The struggles within the community between Orthodox and Zionist were less vehement. In Munkács, there was the militant leadership of Rabbi Spira, fighting not only the Hebrew Gymnasium and its prominent leader Dr. Kugel, but also any other group that might infringe upon his authority. In Ungvár, the rabbinic leadership was less dynamic, which in turn facilitated the liberal spirit, although basically the community was very traditional. There also were good relations between the rabbi and the Orthodox Archbishop of the city who was also the head of the seminary. Each year they issued a joint exhortation to the residents reminding them to observe separation of the sexes while bathing in the river.

The fine relations between Jews and Ruthenians began to deteriorate, however, when the the Czechs opened their schools and universities to the young Ruthenians, providing them with educational opportunities that had never been available under Hungarian rule. Thus the economic and social struggle between the groups began, later to become intensified during the 1930's. The problem of poverty was very much on the agenda of the government authorities. These were the depression years, and they were particularly tragic for the Jews. In the rural areas they were accused of exploiting the peasants by supplying them with alcohol and loans at exorbitant rates, while in the towns Jewish shopkeepers were charged with being "aliens," who ruined their Christian competitors by driving down prices. As so often before, the Jews were made the scapegoats for generally deteriorating conditions that caused strikes, grain shortages and widespread starvation. The situation is best described by citing part of Dr. Kugel's 1935 speech to Parliament. He had moved from being head of the Hebrew Gymnasium and a minority rights champion to a position of national importance, which was recognized by his election to the Parliament in Prague. This is what he had to say about Subcarpathian Ruthenia:

> If the years preceding the economic crisis were bad, today it is completely impossible to adequately describe the poverty in this area. The Jews who number one-seventh of the total population of the region are affected equally with the rest. Particularly in the rural area, their fate is in no way better than that of non-Jews. I strongly wish to protest against any attempt to blame the poverty of the Subcarpathian Ruthenian peasantry on the Jews. Such accusations are malicious gossip; were their fabricators to visit the Jewish houses in the villages and look at the land registries, they would see for themselves how many Jews have been forced to sell their last possessions to stay alive. The fact that a few Jews receive concessions for the sale of alcohol does not mean that the masses of their fellow Jews are benefited by it, and if some obtain these licenses by means of bribes, one must recall that this was the accepted practice under the old Hungarian regime. Our party, and all who wish to improve the existence of the Jews in this country, to educate them, to render them productive and teach them mutual cooperation, are adamantly opposed to this state of affairs. The economic crisis, which was heightened in the Carpathians by the collapse of the lumber industry and its associated occupations, has had its inevitable effects on the region's Jews, who were already living in great poverty and hardship. Hundreds of Jewish laborers, wagoners and hired hands remain without jobs. Due to the flight of industry, hundreds of skilled Jewish workers have been deprived of their livelihood.[25]

The Jews were not the only ones who were dissatisfied with the government. The Ruthenians, with their large peasant constituency, suffered intensely from the general depression. Moreover, they were still trying to acquire the autonomous status promised them since the beginning of the Czech administration. This discontent was fanned by the Hungarians in and out of Subcarpathian Ruthenia who were interested in revising the Trianon Treaty of 1920 and retrieving the territories lost under its provisions. The Polish government under Marshal Pilsudski also declared its support for Hungary's territorial claims. Another and ultimately more decisive threat emanated from Nazi Germany, which clamored for the rights of the German minority living in the Sudetenland, the Western part of Czechoslovakia.

While rightfully complaining about the economic situation, the Jews were fully aware that their hopes lay with the continuation of the Czech government. This was clearly expressed in December 1935, when Thomas G. Masaryk resigned from the presidency of Czechoslovakia due to advanced age and was succeeded by Dr. Eduard Benes, the longtime foreign minister of the republic. When the representatives of the Jewish party offered their congratulations to the new President on April 22, 1936, stating that they considered his election a victory for the ideals of democracy, Benes replied, "You know what my policy was towards the Jewish Renaissance movement while I was Minister for Foreign Affairs. I want to assure you that I will continue to pursue the same policy in my new position. The creation of a Jewish National Home will have a salutary effect on the position of Jews all over the world and will serve to end, or at least to mitigate, the hardships which the Jews are suffering in many countries."[26] At this occasion the delegation handed the new President a memorandum that expressed hope that he would support the Hebrew school system and the democratization of election by-laws for the Jewish religious congregations. Without mentioning any specific names, the hope of the Jewish party leaders representing Zionist sentiments was that the President would support them in their struggle against Rabbi Spira and his ongoing effort to establish an independent bureau of all Orthodox congregations in the province. The rabbi and his followers wanted to control the type of candidates elected so as to ensure that only Orthodox would be allowed to function. According to the Hungarian law of 1869 still operative in Czechoslovakia, no two communities of the same religious outlook were permitted to exist side by side. This was an outcome of the Jewish Congress of 1868/69, which had been convened by the Hungarian government to establish the rules by which community life was to function. The government had hoped to establish one overall organization; instead, as we have already seen, the Congress led to the establishment of two and sometimes three communal organizations: the Neolog, Orthodox and Status-Quo.[27]

Rabbi Spira and the Munkács Community

Only twice had there been separate communities in Northeastern Hungary, one in Ungvár, which did not last too long, and the other in Sziget, where it endured due to its special history and the fine leadership of its rabbi, Dr. Samuel Danzig.[28] Throughout his life, Rabbi Spira had tried to maintain the Orthodox character of the congregations, despite increasing opposition from local and national forces. In 1927, Moritz Feldinger led 49 members of Munkács's Orthodox congregation applying to the government for permission to form a Neolog community.[29] This formal step of separation followed a long period of antagonism toward the establishment. The opposition must have become more vocal and organized in 1923, when Rabbi Spira forced the expulsion of Rabbi Isachar Dov Rokeach, the Belzer Rebbe. The major violation, with which the opposition was charged, consisted of their appointment of a rabbi (R.S. Grinfeld) and a shochet (ritual slaughterer) of their own. Technically they were in the wrong, for appointment of such officials was the exclusive prerogative of the communal authority vested in Spira. His religious court, led by Rabbi David Schlüssel, not only mobilized many of the Orthodox rabbis of Hungary and Galicia, but even Shlomo Elazar Alfandari, listed as a Chief Rabbi from

Jerusalem. They condemned the new community and warned all the faithful to shun their company and not eat the meat slaughtered by their shochet. In the face of this over-whelming condemnation the chances for a successful sepa-rate community were very slim, and in 1933 it was abolished.

Rabbi Spira's longstanding opposition to the Hebrew Gymnasium became particularly vocal in May of 1935, after Kugel's election to the Czech Parliament as a representative of the Jewish party. On June 21, 1935, Rabbi Spira is quoted in his sermon, "Whosoever sends his children to the accursed Hebrew School shall be wiped out, and shall not be permitted to live to raise his children. The children will not live to see the next year. A Zionist must not be called to the Holy Ark, and no one may partake of his wine. For the past ten years I have spat whenever I passed the Godless Hebrew High School."[30]

The school instituted legal proceedings against the outs-poken rabbi, which at first were dismissed in the District Court of Ungvár. But then the Court of Appeals found him guilty of a misdemeanor, and sentenced him to a fine of 1000 Korunas or twenty days in prison.

Rabbi Spira died in 1937, and was succeeded by his son-in-law, Rabbi Baruch Rabinowicz, the husband of his only daughter, Frime. It must be added that Rabbi Spira had been a great scholar who left a number of important Talmudic volumes. He had headed a Yeshivah of more than 200 stu-dents, whom he always called "his children, colleagues and teachers," according to the words of his Testament, drawn up ten years prior to his death.[31] Those who opposed him did so with a passion, but those that followed him respected a dyna-mic leader.[32] A simple listing of the Jewish societies will show the intensity of communal life within Munkács, where in 1930, 11,313 Jews composed 43 per cent of the total popu-lation.

Community Organizations in Munkács
STUDY GROUPS

1. *Chevrat Machzike Torah* (Supporters of Torah)
   Administered the religious education program for students up to age 14.

2. *Chevrat Tamchin De'Orayta* (Supporters of Torah Study)
   Provided funds for education of poor children from Hasidic homes.

3. *Chevrat Talmud Torah* (Supporters of Study of Torah)
   Provided funds for education of poor from non-Hasidic homes.

4. *Chevrat Tiferet Bachurim* (Pride of Young Men)
   Group of young employees within the business community who gathered evenings, Sabbath and Holidays to study.

5. *Chevrat Tanach* (Bible Study Group)
   Association of young business people who met to study the weekly Scripture readings.

6. *Chevrah L'Kinyan Ve'Tikun Sefarim* (Society for the Purchase and Repair of Religious Books)
   Each synagogue, which also served as a House of Study, had a group buying and repairing books for prayer and study.

7. *Chevrah Likute Shemot* (Society for the Collection of Worn-out Pages)
   The purpose of this group was to collect stray pages of worn-out books lying about in the streets. Poor people used to collect them in bags for which they received payment.

8. *Chevrah Mishnayot* (Society for the Study of the Mishnah)
   Each Synagogue and *Bet Midrash* had groups to study the Oral Law in memory of the departed.

9. *Yeshivah Darke Teshuvah* (Talmudical Academy, "Ways of Repentance")
    More than 200 students, aged 14 and upward, under the leadership of Rabbi Chaim Elazar Spira.

CHARITABLE SOCIETIES

Chevrah Kadisha (Holy Burial Society)
An almost autonomous institution for the purpose of preparing and burying the dead.

Chevrat Tzedakah Vachesed (Society for Charity and Kindness)
Society to help the poor in a discreet manner.

Chevrat Poale Tzedek (Society of Doers of Justice)
Society to support impoverished artisans.

Chevrat Gemilut Chasadim (Society for the Dispensation of Good Deeds)
Society for lending money without interest, particularly to artisans and young businessmen.

Chevrat Bikur Cholim (Society for Visitations to the Sick)
Purpose: to visit the sick and assist with medicine and doctors.

Chevrat Hachnasat Kallah (Brides' Fund)
Purpose: to help poor brides.

In the field of welfare, two additional women's groups functioned: one to care for the soup kitchen and another for poor women in confinement.

The American Joint Distribution Committee was helpful in the following organizations of its own:

1. Cooperative bank for loans with an accompanying relief fund.
2. Assistance to orphans.
3. Training school for poor girls.

The above organizations are described in detail to show the

extent to which the Munkács Jewish community was organized. While other, smaller communities throughout the region were not as diversified, they operated under the same
principles of mutual responsibility and help for each Jew.
The concept of government support for social welfare and
education was something new that developed rather slowly
after World War I, when a liberal Czech government tried to
live up to its promises of minority rights.

The great variety of educational activities witnessed in
Munkács and these other communities reflects the emphasis
Judaism has always placed on education and learning. To the
religious Jew, life is an unbroken chain of study and commit-
ment. One of the distinguishing attributes of the rabbis we
have met—and we have only met a few—was the titles of the
scholarly books that they wrote. Often these rabbis are—and
were—better known by their book titles than by their own
family names. Another characteristic was the Yeshivah they
headed—the number of students that they taught. And if the
rabbi had a following of Hasidim who traveled from near and
far to be with him, then he wore the triple crown of duties:
Communal Rabbi, Head of a Yeshivah and Leader of Hasidim.
This triple crown (the term "crown" is used advisedly because many "calls" to serve contain Hebrew phrases, e.g.
"Come, be a King over us")was worn by the more important
rabbis of northeastern Hungary. They developed into dynasties, often with much pomp and circumstance, passsing on
their figurative crowns to their children or nearest relatives.
This applies to the Spiras of Munkács, the Teitelbaums of
Sziget and Szatmár, the Hagers of Vishnitz and the Weiss' of
Spinka. It should be emphasized that the rabbis from these
dynasties had to undergo rigorous training by their learned
elders; and while the positions came to them by virtue of their
family, the quality of their leadership and learning remained
an individual achievement. All these Hasidic leaders
frowned on secular studies, which they considered an in-
terference with and danger to religious life. When the Hunga-

rian government instituted compulsory education, they made private arrangements for schooling in compliance with the law. This applies particularly to Pressburg, the most famous Yeshivah of Hungary, which was the only one officially recognized by the government to grant rabbinical ordination.[33] Private ordination was widely practiced in Hasidic circles. Neolog congregations obtained their rabbis from graduates of the theological seminaries of Budapest, Vienna and various cities in Germany.

Rumania's Rule in Máramaros

At this juncture in our story we have to cross the border from Czechoslovakia into Rumania. We already have seen that this country, like Czechoslovakia, played an active role in Subcarpathian Ruthenia during World War I. There had been a small number of Rumanians living in this part of Hungary, which gave their claim for territory a certain legitimacy. The allies, however, rejected their claim for all of Máramaros county. Only the area south of the river Tisa was ceded to Rumania, led at the time of the Paris Peace Conference by Prime Minister Ionel Bratianu. Ever since the Congress of Berlin in 1878, when Rumanian independence was achieved, this country had been slow in granting its Jews full civil rights. When Bratianu appeared in Paris, Georges Clemenceau, the great French leader, reminded him of his country's failings. To avoid further violations, the Great Powers (France, England and the United States) decided to include provisions in the treaty, guaranteeing political rights to the Jews. This was most important since the new territories acquired by Rumania included the provinces of Bukovina, Bessarabia and Transylvania, all of which had very large Jewish populations.[34] Our major concern is with Northern Transylvania, whose community of Sziget we already have met. The rabbi serving this community during the trying years of World War I was Chaim Tzvi Teitelbaum, who held office from 1904 to 1926. He continued in the sacred tradition of his family to provide leadership to a community full of scholars, Hasidic rabbis and tradition-oriented Jews. In 1910, approximately 8,000 Jews lived in Sziget, 35 per cent of the total population. The city's people and economy were very similar to those of other towns in mountainous Máramaros. We quote from a memorandum of March 20, 1920, written by the Jewish National Organization of Máramaros to the General Jewish Relief Conference of Zurich, Switzerland:[35]

> The Máramaros Jews distinguish themselves particularly through their conservative, strongly Jewish character, strong physique and their sane though simpler viewpoint, as well as their ability and willingness to work . . . Perhaps they are the only Jews in the Diaspora who can show so high a percentage of small farmers. This occupation not only makes them especially fit for colonizing Palestine, but also because they look upon the National idea with such favor. . . . The Máramaros Jewish wood and forest workers enjoy the best reputation at home and abroad. . . . Among the large number of artisans they have tanners, smiths, locksmiths and bricklayers as well as agricultural workers and carpenters; cabinetmakers deserve special mention. There are also a large number of superior tailors and cobblers. . . . Because of lack of time and the existing political conditions we are unfortunately not in a position to give exact statistical data. For the same reasons we cannot furnish data about the many thousands of war orphans, widows and prisoners as well as the immeasurable damage which our brethren suffered. We only wish to point out the fact that our country was a battleground during the entire duration of the War, and that the enemy as well as our soldiers discharged their special fury against the Jews. The Russian invasion caused our brethren great misery and to this must be added the fact that our poor Jews evacuated their homes and had to abandon their property to the enemy. The pogroms at the time of the Revolution also occurred here, although we had organized a Jewish guard for the defense of Jewish property and Jewish blood, which soon re-established order. All this had a paralyzing effect on trade and the merchant class as well as the artisans, who all suf-

fered greatly under these trials. . . . The Máramaros Jews stand before an economic crisis, if not before the total ruin, as it possesses neither raw materials nor opportunity for work. A national relief is therefore of very urgent necessity.

The memorandum closed by recommending the establishment of a central credit association with a network of branches throughout the province to provide long-term credits to farmers and artisans. It also urged the creation of agricultural and trade schools to train adults in useful vocations, as well as a commission to study the human resources of the region. The report was signed by Dr. Illés Blank and Mór Edelstein.

Alexander A. Landesco, who visited Rumania on behalf of the Joint early in 1920 made similar findings. Despite the great need, however, only two local committees were established, one in Sziget and another in Cluj, a paucity that reflected the lack of communal experience in the region's cities. The committees served as agencies to distribute relief sent from the Jews in the United States to relatives in the area. This was very helpful in that the Joint's major effort in Rumania had to be concentrated on the many thousands of refugees who had poured into Bessarabia from the Ukraine. Even so, the Joint was very active in organizing summer colonies for needy children in Tihata, Sziget and Szatmár. This program began in 1922, and still was going strong in 1936 with plans for future years on the drawing board. While well conceived, the memorandum's call for establishment of a bank took a few years until realization. Many legal hurdles had to be overcome in order to create the financial institution, the so-called "Loan Kassa," which began functioning in 1926. By 1930, a total of 12 *kassas* operated throughout Transylvania, four of them situated in Sziget itself. These *kassas* proved very worthwhile to all their members who, by 1933, had risen to close to 14,000 with over $150,000 in deposits. Approximately 50 per cent of the loans were given to traders and merchants, 25 percent to artisans and small manufacturers and the remaining 25 per cent to a group listed in the statistics as "others," meaning farmers, employees and those in the free professions. The average loan was approximately $50, an indication that the *kassas* were helpful to modest income people in need of small sums of cash. Most of the loans were repaid in the same year, with some borrowers receiving loans two and three times each year, usually after the previous loan had been repaid. One more statistic establishing the value of these credit cooperatives: in 1929, 17,354 loans were granted throughout Transylvania, amounting to close to $800,000.

The Sziget Community and the Teitelbaum Dynasty

The years between World War I and II were marked by some very interesting developments in the life of Sziget.[36] In 1919, a Jewish school was organized by the Zionist leaders with Hebrew as the basic language of instruction. There were four classes for boys and girls, with the number of students rising to 130. By 1924, however, the school had to be closed due to lack of funds as well as that of popular support. It must be kept in mind that Sziget was basically a Hasidic community with a strongly anti-Zionist leadership. Only gradually did religious Zionism in the form of the Mizrachi organization make its influence felt. However, anti-Zionism was not the only obstacle towards a Hebrew language school system as had developed across the border in communities such as Munkács and Ungvár, now under Czech rule; the major stumbling block was the Rumanian government itself. Until 1925, this government did not recognize the graduation certificates of Jewish schools, and all pupils had to pass state examinations, which in the case of the poor were paid from the community budget. After 1925, Jewish school certificates were recognized only if the language of instruction was Rumanian. This official policy was contrary to the agreement signed by the Rumanian government after World War I, which stipulated the rights of the minorities in all the areas annexed by the Rumanians. The Jews of Sziget, who were mainly Yiddish and Hungarian speaking, suffered from this disregard of their rights. In 1923, the Rumanian government finally introduced laws into the constitution allowing for the granting of citizenship to Jews living in the annexed territories. But soon thereafter, they issued administrative restrictions that curtailed the basic rights of citizenship.

A very upsetting event occurred in the internal life of Sziget, when Chaim Tzvi Teitelbaum died in 1926 at the age of 46, having been the communal rabbi for 22 years. His early death created a serious question as to the choice of a successor, for at the time the rabbi's oldest son, Yekutiel Yehuda, was merely fourteen years old and unable, as well as reluctant, to step into his late father's position. All reports about Chaim Tzvi describe him as an even-tempered scholar, very much beloved by the hundreds of students of his Yeshivah.[37] One solution to the problem of successorship presented itself in the person of Rabbi Yoel Teitelbaum, the young man's uncle, then 40 years of age. He enjoyed a fine reputation and had a large following of Hasidim of his own. How did it happen that 14-year-old Yekutiel Yehuda became the new communal rabbi? To appreciate more fully the dilemma of the community, we must briefly sketch Rabbi Yoel's history up to that year.

Yoel was eighteen when his own father died in 1904. The position of communal leadership passed to his older brother, Chaim Tzvi, and Rabbi Yoel moved to Szatmár, about 60 miles west of Sziget. Shortly beforehand, he had married the daughter of the Rebbe of Plontsh of the House of Horowitz, another Hasidic dynasty.[38] Szatmár, at the time of his arrival, was served by Rabbi Yehuda Grünwald, a disciple of the Pressburg Yeshivah, who was much dedicated to education of the young. He was succeeded in 1921 by Rabbi Eliezer Grünwald (no relation), a very learned scholar, whose fine leadership attracted three to five hundred Yeshivah students at various times. Rabbi Teitelbaum did not remain in Szatmár for long—there was only a small group of Hasidim in town—

but moved in 1911 to Urshava in Subcarpathian Ruthenia, where he soon made a name for himself through his learning, piety and strict interpretation of the law. He followed the rules laid down by the Chatam Sofer (Rabbi Moses Schreiber of Pressburg) in the early 19th century, forbidding any changes within Jewish ritual. It is small wonder that he should have become an adversary of Zionist ideologies, but even more, he refused to join the Orthodox party, *Agudath Israel*, although it too fought against the secular concepts of Zionism.

The fiery proponent of this stand against Agudath Israel was, of course, Rabbi Chaim Elazar Spira of Munkács. In 1921, Spira had visited Rabbi Abraham Mordecai Alter (1866-1948), also known as the Gerer Rebbe, one of the greatest Hasidic leaders of Poland. As the Gerer Rebbe had been one of the founders of Agudath Israel, Rabbi Spira had tried unsuccessfully to influence him to change his views. Upon his return, Rabbi Spira called a meeting of rabbis, which took place in the summer of 1922 in Cop, to argue against any involvement with the Agudath Israel party. At this gathering, Yoel Teitelbaum strongly endorsed Spira's views, stating that "some of the present Orthodox community leaders were not always strong in their faith . . . the only way to preserve our Torah is by uniting with like-minded people in our own congregations, and not with large groups in faraway places . . ." It is interesting that Yoel Teitelbaum's arguments were similar to those of Rabbi Spira, who struggled for an independent Orthodox community organization in Subcarpathian Ruthenia. By the time of his brother's death in 1926, Yoel Teitelbaum had become an important leader with a large following, but his views may have been too extreme to make him acceptable to the leaders of Sziget.[39]

After World War I, there had been a trend towards greater freedom of thought and action within the community. While it is difficult to measure change within such a short period, a few dates stand out, mainly involving the young and the intelligentsia. There was the initial founding of a primary school in 1920 with Hebrew as the language of instruction; although it had to be discontinued in 1924, its existence reflects the new spirit. The prime mover behind this nationalist effort was Dr. Eliyahu Blank, an attorney who ultimately went to Palestine in 1926. Then, there was the program of trade schools and apprentices' homes, in which the Joint was very much involved all throughout Transylvania. The combination of scholarly Yeshivah study with vocational training made this effort even more noticeable, almost revolutionary. The concept of supplementing the exclusively religious Yeshivah studies with practical courses that would enable the student to make a living had been in the air for a while.[40] It was Rabbi Yekutiel Yehuda Gross of Sziget, however, who put it into practice for the first time in 1928. The scheme, supported not only by the Joint, but also by other organizations, worked as follows. Students, 18 years of age, who had excelled in their studies were permitted to take weaving courses that were given six hours daily and lasted for two years. The remainder of the day was devoted to religious studies. Each student received 40 per cent of his earnings, while the balance was kept in escrow until his marriage. This would enable him to open a weaving shop. Rabbi Gross wanted to introduce additional courses for jewelry making and watch repairs. He also planned to buy land for vegetable farming and milk production. These far-reaching plans were brought to a halt, however, by the outbreak of World War II and the Holocaust. Rabbi Gross had to battle his fellow rabbis for his new ideas; they called him the "Red Rabbi" in spite of the fact that he was one of the most pious Hasidic leaders in the community. Had Yoel Teitelbaum become the communal Rabbi of Sziget, men like Rabbi Gross certainly would have been unable to put such new ideas into practice.

It must also be kept in mind that there were many other Hasidic groups in the city, among them the Vishnitzer, Bel-

zer, Doliner, Kossover and Spinker Hasidim. They all had
rebbes and places of worship of their own. While we do not
have statistics for each group, we know that Sziget's Jewish
population had risen in 1930 to approximately 11,000 which
represented 40 per cent of the total inhabitants. During Holiday time when many Hasidim from outside Sziget came to
visit their rebbes, the numbers grew much larger. The fact
that in 1926 the community could agree on the election of a
fourteen-year-old indicates that its structure was strong
enough to carry on without a mature leader.

A great deal of this strength was vested in the Bet Din, the
religious court, that discharged a large share of the daily
duties of running a Jewish community. This, of course, was
not always to the satisfaction of its constituents. Take for
example the court's edict forbidding the import of meat that
was slaughtered outside Sziget. As we have seen previously,
the communal budget depended to a large degree upon the
taxes derived from the slaughter of animals and sale of meat.
When local meat became more expensive, due to an increase
in taxes, many began buying it from outside communities
where prices were lower. While meat was a necessity, it was
also a great luxury for the thousands of Sziget Jews who, for
the most part, were poor. The champion in the fight against
the ban was Rabbi Israel Weiss, a very wealthy resident who
organized large demonstrations against the Bet Din and its
ban. The court reacted strongly, placing guards throughout
the city to prevent the bringing in of outside meat. Moreover,
it declared Weiss unfit to hold public office for the next five
years.[41] This whole struggle shows the determination of the
Bet Din to maintain its authority and to guarantee the fiscal
solvency of the community.

Theoretically the communal rabbi was also the head of
the Bet Din. Thus, the election of the fourteen-year-old Yekutiel Yehudah Teitelbaum must be viewed largely as a symbol
of the continuity of the Teitelbaum dynasty. The members of
the court were all senior rabbis whose scholarship and ex-

perience guided the young rabbi in his decisions. This may be seen from another event whereby he was approached to permit the formation of an Agudath Israel youth group. It was argued that there was a need for the young people to belong to a party which was supported by the leading Orthodox Rabbis of the land and had branches all over Europe.[42] The *Gabbai* (rabbi's aide) advised against approval for fear that the more militant Hasidim would object to any involvement with Agudath Israel. This advice prevented an official endorsement, but the young rabbi quietly promised help once things became more settled. This was enough to allow the formation of the first Agudath Israel youth group in Sziget in 1931.

Of course it would have been unthinkable for Rabbi Teitelbaum to support the Mizrachi even in the slightest as long as it advocated a brand of Zionism, albeit based on religious concepts. but even the strongest opposition of the establishment could not prevent the growth of the Mizrachi movement in Transylvania. This was due largely to the leadership of Rabbi Samuel Glasner, who served the important community of Klausenburg from 1878 until 1922. He was a great scholar and had participated in the first Mizrachi world conference at Pressburg in 1904. He also had been a Mizrachi delegate at the 12th Zionist Congress which took place in Carlsbad in 1921.[43] In Sziget itself, the leader of the movement was none other than Dr. Samuel Danzig, whose Sephardic community had been a symbol of opposition to the establishment since the 1880's. When the first convention of the Mizrachi party of Transylvania took place in Sziget in 1929, it was attended by Rabbi Meir Berlin, the party's world leader. Another leader, Rabbi Yehuda Leib Fishman, visited Sziget in 1931. What may come as a surprise, however, is the fact that Sziget even had a Hasidic Rebbe, Yoseph Lichtenstein, who had his own following and who preached the idea of a state for the Jewish people.

Of the many outstanding personalities from this period, one deserves special mention. It is Rabbi Leopold Greenwald,

born in Sziget in 1889, a descendant of a distinguished rabbinic family and a graduate of the famous Pressburg Yeshivah. Although already in his 30's, he decided to seek a life in
freedom by immigrating to the United States where he served
as a rabbi at Columbus, Ohio, from 1924 to 1955, making it a
stronghold of traditional Judaism. A great Talmudic scholar,
he corresponded with the leading rabbinic authorities of his
time. Very much interested in Jewish history, particularly
that of Hungary, he wrote extensively on this subject. A
champion of the religious Zionist movement, he was also
very active in communal affairs. During World War II he
marched in Washington, petitioning President Roosevelt to
save European Jewry from destruction by the Nazis. Upon his
demise, he left a rich legacy of 44 scholarly books and numerous articles on a wide range of Jewish subjects.[44]

There are others from the Carpathian mountain region
who became well-known for literary and journalistic en-
deavors. Naphtali Ben–Menachem (formerly Fried) was born
1911 in Havasmezö, near Sziget, and lived in Israel from 1935
until his death in 1976.[45] He wrote extensively on Hebrew
books and manuscripts. Of special value to our story is his
Hebrew volume on Hungarian Jewish literature[46] in which he
carefully describes the 186 books and 17 newspapers that
were published in Sziget between 1874 and 1942. They are
ample proof of the scholarly climate and alert reading public
within the community.

From a historical perspective, the newspapers are of
special interest because they reveal the struggle of new ideas
and the often tortuous path towards greater intellectual freedom. The pioneer of Hebrew newspaper publishing was Abraham Ginzler. His weekly *Hator* (The Line) appeared off and
on between 1874 and 1876. After him comes Hirsch Leib
Gottlieb whose story is already known to us. His progressive
views, as expressed in his shortlived Hebrew weekly *Hashemesh* (The Sun), which appeared between 1878 and 1880,
brought him into conflict with the Hasidic establishment and

forced him to continue his writing and publishing in the more liberal climate of Kolomea, Galicia. Thinking that a Yiddish weekly would be more acceptable in Sziget, he published from 1893 to 1897 his *Yiddishe Volkszeitung* (Jewish People's Paper). Again he met with a ban by Chananya Yom Tov Lipa Teitelbaum, the communal rabbi. Since the owner of the press, Abraham Kaufman, was also the president of the Orthodox community, the ban was most effective. (It deserves to be mentioned that this press monopoly forced the Sephardic community to publish a volume *Ohev Mishpat* (Lover of Law), which presented its position against the Orthodox community, in Lemberg, Galicia, in 1887. The year before, the case of the Orthodox community had been detailed in the volume, *Milchemet Mitzvah* (Battle of the Commandment), which was of course published in Sziget itself.)

But Gottlieb never gave up. After the rabbi's demise he started his third weekly, the Hebrew language *Zion* (1904-1906), for which Dr. Theodor Herzl had donated the type. To avoid any trouble with the Hasidim, Gottlieb set the type in his own home and brought it under cover of night to the printer. He personally distributed the paper to his readers and even sold copies in the street. As time went by, especially after World War I, more Yiddish papers appeared. There was also a Hungarian-Hebrew monthly *Darkenu* (Our Road), dedicated to the ideals of religious Zionism and edited by M. Kofler, M. Weiss and A. Israel.

In 1930, the Sziget community rejoiced over the simultaneous appearance there of two great personalities.[47] One was Yoseph Holder, the Yiddish writer, who had come from Budapest, Hungary, to visit his parents living in Sziget. The other was Avigdor Hameiri (formerly Feuerstein, 1890-1970) who came from Palestine. A native of Dávidháza in Bereg county, Hameiri had already achieved a fine reputation as a writer, poet and translator. After a traditional Yeshivah education at Pressburg, he had started out as a journalist, soon becoming devoted to the Zionist idea. After service as an officer in the Hungarian army and captivity in Siberia, he went to Israel where he became one of the foremost writers of his generation. Finally, a special role in Sziget's literary world was played by Herzl Apsan, a businessman who turned writer rather late in life. Of his legacy only one volume survives, sufficient to earn him the name of "Sholom Alei-chem" of Sziget.[48] A Vishnitzer Hasid himself, his book, *Beis Yisroel, Vishnitzer Rebbe's Hoyf* (The House of Israel, The Court of the Vishnitzer Rebbe) provides an excellent insight into Hasidic life of his time. Two chapters are translated in the Appendix.

All this community organization and literary expression developed despite difficult economic and political conditions. First, most of the Hungarian economic contacts were cut off when Transylvania was annexed by Rumania after World War I. Then, there was the slow process of naturalization, granting Hungarian-speaking Jews political rights under the new Rumanian government. In December 1922, Christian students at the four Rumanian universities proclaimed a "numerus clausus" aimed at preventing young Jews from pursuing academic careers. These student movements, organized and financed by the Ministry of Interior, resulted not only in riots at the universities, but also against the civilian population in various towns. The leader of the students' league was Corneliu Zelea Codreanu who, in 1929, founded the Iron Guard, a para-military organization with an extreme anti-Semitic program. Two years before, members of this league carried out a pogrom in Oradea Mare (Transylvania) where they were holding a congress subsidized again by the Ministry of Interior. Five synagogues were wrecked and the Torah scrolls burned in the public square. In Cluj, the capital of Transylvania, eight prayer houses were plundered, and excesses were committed in other cities. After Hitler came to power in Germany in 1933, the large Rumanian parties also adopted anti-Semitic programs.

The economic crisis of the early 1930's caused widespread hunger in Sziget and northern Transylvania. Here the Joint made a special effort to save the children from the effects of starvation. They maintained summer camps, in which 1,300 children were fed in 1933, a number that rose to 5,000 in 1935. Thirty per cent of the budget came from Joint sources; the remainder was covered locally. Another source of help were the loan kassas. From 1933 to '37 they were expanded with large sums from the Joint reaching a total of 80 in 1938. About 25 per cent of the total Jewish population was helped by these financial institutions, which proved particularly important at a time when Jewish banks were failing due to the anti-Semitic measures. By 1936 no Jewish lawyers were accepted by the Rumanian bar; by 1937, the last four Jewish students admitted to medical school were prevented by force from attending classes. In 1938, a new government under Octavian Goga began issuing decrees requiring all Jews to establish their residence by documentation. This had never been done before. It was particularly difficult, well-nigh impossible, in the territories that had been acquired by Rumania after World War I. The Peace Treaty had stipulated that residents of these territories would automatically become citizens, but all these promises had long been forgotten. By the end of 1938, the number of Jews who could not document their residence amounted to 150,000. From then on, they were to be considered foreigners who had to obtain certificates of identity authorizing their stay for a year at a time. Licenses for trade, industry or the professions were no longer issued to them. The Rumanian situation had become extremely difficult.

Northeastern Counties of Hungarian Kingdom before 1918.
(*From: Magocsi*, The Shaping of a National Identity)

Subcarpathian border changes, 1938–1945.
(*From: Magocsi*, The Shaping of a National Identity)

3. | THE HOLOCAUST

Destruction of Czechoslovakia

Events in Czechoslovakia were deeply affected by developments across the border in Germany. The consolidation of Hitler's power moved along rather swiftly; the Allies, France and England, stood by silently as he rearmed, moved into the Ruhr and annexed Austria early in 1938. Tragically, Hitler's racial policies against the Jews in Germany, of tremendous concern to Jews everywhere, were considered an internal matter by the Allies. Although these policies were criticized by liberals in and out of the Reich, such talk did not lead to any political action. Perhaps the establishment of a High Commissioner's Office for German Refugees by the League of Nations in the mid-1930's can be considered as an international action, but it is better described as "reaction" and inadequate at that. For it was never strong enough to prevent the flow of refugees or to find sufficient places of refuge. Czechoslovakia, true to its liberal tradition, gave asylum to several thousand persecuted by the Nazis, and the Jewish communities were very active in providing help to transients on the way to Palestine.[1]

As for the Jews of Czechoslovakia themselves, there had only been limited emigration to Palestine from 1920 until the Nazi occupation of Prague, March 15, 1939. This was due to a

number of reasons. While there had been anti-Semitism in
the country ever since Czechoslovakia came into being after
World War I, top government figures, such as Masaryk and
Benes, were among the most liberal and democratic leaders
in Europe. They were the ones who not only promised, but
also provided economic opportunities and political equality
for Jewish citizens. Moreover, Jews of Bohemia, Moravia and
Silesia, also known as the Historic Lands, had been living
there since 960 and had become fully integrated in the
country's development. There was a freedom in the land after
World War I that allowed the establishment of a Jewish party
and a nationalistic movement. Finally, even those who had
wanted to settle in Palestine found it very difficult to obtain
entry, which was based on certificates issued by the British
government. In view of the limited number of certificates,
first priority had to be given to the Jews of Poland, Rumania
and Germany, who were increasingly menaced by persecution. Still, between World Wars I and II approximately 6,000
were issued to qualified immigrants from Czechoslovakia.
There was, in addition, an "illegal immigration" of about the
same number of people down the Danube from Pressburg to
the Black Sea. Here they boarded ships clandestinely to avoid
internment by the British authorities. Thus, the bulk of Czech
Jewry, approximately 350,000 people in 1930, remained in
their native country, hoping that the national borders
separating them from Germany would protect them.[2]

Not only the Jews of the Historic Lands, which were
close to the German border, but also those of Subcarpathian
Ruthenia felt deep concern about the rising menace of
Nazism. As we have seen before, there was still the general
problem of local autonomy for the province as pushed by the
Ruthenians and the issue of the Hebrew school system for
which the Government was asked to provide full financial
support. On January 5, 1937, a Jewish delegation headed by
Dr. Kugel, was received by the Governor who made this
reply:

The population of Subcarpathian Ruthenia is averse to anti-Semitism in every form. There is no fertile ground for Jew-hatred in Subcarpathian Ruthenia, and the fascist elements who want to transplant this bad seed here will fail . . . the autonomy of S.R. will not be to the detriment of any minority. As long as the Governor continues in office—and there is no reason for a change in this respect—he will, by virtue of his authority, put a stop to any excesses of hostility. He will see to it that the Jewish school system will be placed under the care of the State and will be developed as are the Ruthenian schools.[3]

The mood of the Jews at this time is recorded in a statement issued by the Jewish party on May 15, 1938, two months after Hitler's annexation of Austria:

The Jews have fully identified themselves with the Republic. They know very well that they will have to share its fate for better or for worse. Without exception and without reservations, they stand behind the Czecho-Slovak people and the Czecho-Slovak State. They have placed all their moral and economic resources at its disposal and are ready to give their lives and their possessions if need be.

And finally, this proclamation issued on September 30, 1939, the day of the Munich agreement, which tried to buy peace at the expense of the Czech state, but in reality only delayed the showdown between Germany and the Allies for a short year:

Our Republic has been dealt a severe blow. An undeserved grievous wrong has been done to the Czecho-Slovak people. At this moment, we gratefully recall the twenty years of the history of this young state which, in the midst of a world infested with anti-Semitism, invited the Jewish citizens to participate in its peaceful upbuilding and granted them full civil and national rights.

We solemnly reiterate our vow of unchanging love and loyalty to this state, to whose service the Jews will continue to devote the best of their energies. We have faith and confidence in the state and its duly constituted leaders. We have faith in the genius of the Czecho-Slovak people and believe that it will continue unswervingly upon the path of justice and humanity marked out for it by destiny and by its leaders.

At the same time, we are mindful of the bitter fate of our Jewish brethren who are directly and personally affected by this tragic change in our borders. They must now find new work and homes in this State. Bound up with them by destiny as we are, we stand ready to assist them. Together we shall continue to work for our Republic, for the Jewish people and for our Zionist ideas.

The few months between the Munich agreement and the occupation of Czechoslovakia by German troops on March 15, 1939 witnessed the establishment of an autonomous government in Subcarpathian Ruthenia now known as Carpatho-Ukraine.[4] But its leaders' hopes for autonomy were short-lived. The arrival of the German troops in Bohemia and Moravia coincided with the annexation of the province by Hungary, which had given it up only 20 years earlier. Thus the fate of its 100,000 Jews again became intertwined with the fate of all of Hungary's Jewry.

Hungary's Annexation of Subcarpathian Ruthenia

The annexation of Subcarpathian Ruthenia by Hungary increased pressure on Jewish leaders to find opportunities for emigration. In April, 1939, the chairman of the Orthodox community in Ungvár, Dr. Julius Lászlo, went to London with the approval of the Hungarian authorities to seek help in two areas: first, to investigate the possibility for group settlement in the British Colonies of several hundred Jewish farm families; second, to submit a memorandum to the British Foreign Office in which he appealed for intercession with the Polish authorities on behalf of approximately 3,000 Jews of Polish origin. These were individuals living in Subcarpathian Ruthenia who had lost their Polish citizenship because they had been living outside Poland for more than five years.

László's mission failed in spite of the fact that outstanding Jewish leaders in Britain had given him full support. Zionist leaders also tried to obtain certificates directly for distribution in Munkács, and not by way of the Central Office in Budapest. But these efforts did not produce significant results.

Hungary already possessed a long history of anti-Semitism. An anti-Jewish party existed in the 1880's, which could be viewed "as an expression of the deep resentment felt by parts of the dispossessed gentry, and the conservative middle-class urban elements against the new capitalist order of which the Jews were considered the mainstay."[5] As a result of the Trianon Peace Treaty of 1920, Hungary had lost two thirds of her territory and more than 60 per cent of her population.[6] The turbulent period after World War I saw the rise of Béla Kun's Communist regime, which had some nominal Jews in its ranks. In reaction, the "White Terror," carried out by army officers under Admiral Miklós Horthy, later Regent of Hungary, killed a few thousand Jews under the pretense that they had been Communist sympathizers. The Jews also were accused of being a harmful political and economic influence, who had led Hungary to war and defeat. Hungary's Jewish population resided predominantly in the cities: more than 200,000, almost half the Jews in Hungary lived in the Greater Budapest area; the rest in smaller cities throughout the land. The only way to Hungary's recovery after World War I was in its industrial and commercial development, areas in which Jews had been most active and successful. This had resulted in a high percentage of Jewish professionals, who were a thorn in the side of many Hungarians. Thus, in 1920, one of the first regulations to be promulgated limited the quota of Jewish university students to 6 per cent (numerus clausus), based on the ratio of the Jewish population of the country. While in the past, Hungary had considered the Jews a religious group, now the law included the terms "race and nationality." This was intended to prevent their escape from Judaism through conversion. Thus, long before the 1939 Nuremberg laws of Hitler, Hungary had established policies that were a gross violation of the principle of equality. The pressure on Jews increased with the rising tide of Nazism in Germany, which found a parallel in the formation of the Arrow-Cross party in Hungary. This party made the solution to the so-called "Jewish question" a major issue, leading to passage of the "first Jewish law" in May 1938. This law limited the percentage of Jews in the professions and economic life to 20 per cent on official grounds that Jewish expansion was harmful to the nation and must be checked. A few months later the "second Jewish law" was passed, further limiting Jews to 6 per cent in the professions and economic life. It also included all persons who had been converted to Christianity after August 1, 1919, approximately 100,000 individuals.

Jewish Labor Units

Special legislation also was passed dealing with the armed forces, which, in the long run, became one of the most brutal acts of anti-Semitism. This legislation stipulated that all persons between the ages of fourteen and seventy were liable to work for the defense of the nation as much as their physical and mental capacities allowed. This harmless and even patriotic sounding phrase was further detailed by another phrase stating that all Hungarian citizens 21 years and older who were classified as "permanently unsuitable" for military service could be compelled to engage in "public labor service" in special camps. While the term "permanently unsuitable" did not specifically allude to Jews, further interpretation clearly indicated thus. From the beginning, conditions in the Jewish labor service companies were tough. At first, service companies were mainly engaged in work within the country, such as road construction, the dredging and clearing of rivers, the unloading of freight in rail yards and the building and maintenance of airfields. Then, in June

1941, when Hungary joined Germany in its invasion of Russia, conditions worsened. The companies were sent to war
zones in the Ukraine where they suffered tremendously from
lack of food and clothing. To quote Professor Braham,[7] the
foremost authority of recent Hungarian Jewish history:

> They had been engaged in strenuous physical activities and
> in long marches that damaged or destroyed their clothes.
> Moreover, many of these companies were under the com-
> mand of especially sadistic officers and guards who subjected
> the servicemen to 'calisthenics' (leap-frogging, somersault-
> ing, crawling, etc.) after they finished work. Frequently, these
> officers denied the servicemen their official food rations,
> which were already inadequate for the hard labor expected,
> and in fact, exacted from them. To survive, many servicemen
> were constantly driven to sell their clothes either to more
> fortunate comrades who had some money, or to the local
> population for food.

Before we continue with the horrible story of the Jewish
labor units, we must realize that by January 1941, Hungary's
Jewish population had increased by approximately 250,000
to a total of approximately 725,000. This was due to the
annexation of Subcarpathian Ruthenia on March 15, 1939
from Czechoslovakia (100,000 Jews) and Northern Transylvania from Rumania on August 30, 1940 (150,000 Jews).[8]
These areas with their large cities of Ungvár, Munkács and
Sziget, had been part of Hungary prior to the Trianon Treaty
of 1920, and their return had been one of the prime objectives
of Hungarian politics since then. Whatever their shaky economic positions may have been, all now grew worse. The
new rulers were looking for Czech and Rumanian sympathizers; again they focused on Jews. As we have seen, the bulk of
these Jews were Orthodox—Hasidic, Yiddish-speaking, descendants of immigrants from Galicia. The assimilated Jews
of Central Hungary looked down upon them, considering
them socially inferior and of little credit to the community at
large.[9] Among the Orthodox were many who had fled from

Poland as a result of the persecution at the end of World War
I, and had remained. There also were many who had settled
in Hungary prior to World War I but somehow did not have
any documentary proof of their Hungarian citizenship. At
first, Hungarian authorities were more understanding but
with Hungary's entry into the war against Russia, approximately 35,000 of these "alien" Jews, mostly in Subcarpathian
Ruthenia, were rounded up and interned. In July 1941, about
20,000 of them were deported across the border to Galicia,
where they were taken over by the Germans and interned in
ghettos. A month later, approximately 14,000 to 16,000 of
these internees were massacred at Kamenets-Podolsk in Eastern Galicia. German SS units, Ukrainian militiamen and
Hungarian troops, in cold blood, machine-gunned innocent
men, women and children. Although the Nazis had taken
measures to conceal these killings, there were too many wit-
nesses who reported these murders to Jewish leaders.[10]

In 1942, the Second Hungarian Army moved into the
Ukraine in support of the German offensive against Russia.
Approximately 50,000 Jews in the labor service units were
attached to this army. The losses suffered by March 1944
were estimated at 42,000, as the Russian winter, the building
of fortifications in icy conditions and the clearing of mine-
fields exacted a heavy toll.[11] On many occasions, the men not
only were told to assist the horse-drawn supply trains, but
often forced to replace the horses that had died from exhaustion. Some particularly anti-Semitic commanders made them
pull heavily-laden wagons, "to save the energy of the animals."[12] Several unbelievable stories are reported by Braham: There were the guards, who amused themselves by
hosing the Jews in winter until they became "ice statues." Or
a situation whereby men, ill with typhoid, were ordered to
run for fifteen minutes together with their healthy comrades,
then "bathe" in the ice-cold river and stand naked in the
wind for inspection by the guards. The following atrocity
even caused the Minister of Defense to order an investigation.

Since many hundreds of Jews suffered from typhoid, a make-shift quarantine "hospital" was set up in the village of Doro-shich, west of Kiev, in the Ukraine. The hospital consisted of a few rooms in a brick building, with most of the patients lying in open barns. Dozens died daily and the corpses were piled up at the wall of a nearby stable. On April 30, 1943, one of the barns with 600 patients was set aflame. The living torches that sprang out of the barn trying to escape were cut down by machine-gun fire of the Hungarian guards.

One of the saddest chapters of the labor service was the killing of about 6,000 Jews, who had been sent to work in the Bor mines of Yugoslavia. It was from there that Germany received about 50 percent of its copper supplies. With the Eastern front collapsing, the Germans were forced to evacu-ate the area and began marching the labor companies back to Hungary. Those that did not die from exhaustion on the march were sent to several concentration camps in Austria and Germany.

Deportations to Auschwitz

These deportations were actually a part of a larger scheme called "The Final Solution" that had been under discussion between Germany and Hungary ever since Miklós Kállay became head of the Hungarian Government on March 7, 1942. The Germans were pushing the Hungarians to elimi-nate the Jews of Hungary, according to their own pernicious plans. Kállay himself was not enough of a Hitler follower to accept the Nazi plans without reservations. He favored the removal of Hungary's Jewry through resettlement after the conclusion of the war. To him, the Jewish question was an internal affair. The Nazis, however, were not pleased with Hungary's policies; they were concerned that Hungary would follow the example of Italy, which had left the Nazi partnership in July of 1943. With the Allied armies advanc-ing successfully on various fronts, Hungary became an un-certain quantity in the Hitler strategy. Hence, the Nazis began

preparing for a total occupation by German troops, which
occurred March 19, 1944, leading to the downfall of Kállay's
Government.[13] At that time, the number of Jews totaled
762,007, of whom 231,453 lived in the Budapest area,
229,318 in the provinces and 301,236 in Subcarpathian Ruthenia and Transylvania. When Hungary was finally liberated by the Allies on April 4, 1945, 618,007 had been deported, killed or died; almost half of these losses, 292,236,
had been suffered by Jews from the annexed areas. It would
seem from these figures that up until the German occupation,
Kállay's policies had enabled the bulk of Hungary's Jewish
population to survive. This is not to say that these policies
were not anti-Semitic. The various anti-Jewish laws, the deportation of the "alien" Jews in 1942, the inhuman treatment
of the labor service companies at the front, all these had taken
a heavy toll. But the extermination of more than 600,000 was
ultimately the crime of the Germans, although the Hungarian
authorities cooperated fully in this "Final Solution."[14] How
was this inhuman feat accomplished? The key executor of the
policy was Adolf Eichmann with his "specially trained"
gangs. It involved three operations: 1) marking the Jews, 2)
placing them into ghettos and 3) deporting them "upon request of the local authorities." The "highlights" of the "Final
Solution" are so abominable, that the pen almost refuses to
write down some of the details. On March 31, all Jews were
ordered to wear the Yellow Badge (Star of David). On April 7,
the decision was reached to place them into ghettos. Local
authorities were confidentially notified of the government's
intention "to clear the country of Jews within a short time."
Braham writes,

> ... the Jews were to be rounded up on a territorial basis
> without regard to sex or age, and would be allowed to take
> along only a minimal amount of supplies: the clothes they
> wore, two sets of underwear and shirts, a fourteen-day supply
> of food, and other baggage not to exceed a total of 50 kilo-
> grams. They were not to be permitted to take along money,

jewelry, gold or other valuables ... On April 1944, i.e. immediately before the evacuation, Carpatho-Ruthenia and Transylvania were declared 'operational zones' so as to justify the 'removal of possible collaborators with the enemy.'

The evacuation of the Jews from their homes, and their placement in the ghettos was carried out by the Hungarian police and gendarmerie under the command of Lt. Col. László Ferenczy, with the collaboration of the Eichmann Sonderkommando. The Jews were aroused in the early morning hours, given only a few minutes to pack their bundles, and then driven into their local synagogues. There they were deprived of all their valuables and began the long sequence of suffering that for most of them ended in the gas chambers of Auschwitz. Their homes were most often left unlocked and looted shortly after their forced departure.

The first to be affected were Jews in the villages of Carpatho-Ruthenia, who were rounded up during the first day of Passover and marched under the most cruel circumstances into areas designated as ghettos in the cities with large Jewish populations. The ghettos themselves were established near the railroad stations, so as to facilitate subsequent deportations.

In Carpatho-Ruthenia the following ghettos were established: Munkács, Kassa, Ungvár, Huszt, Nagyszöllös and Beregszász. In Northern Transylvania the Jewish population was concentrated in two ghettos, in Máramarossziget and Felsövisó. The following is quoted from Braham's account of the Munkács ghetto, which may serve as a sample of the general situation:

Conditions within the boardwall enclosed ghetto were deplorable: food supply was insufficient, sanitation facilities were absent, hospitals and drugs were nonexistent and diseases such as dysentery, typhoid and spotted fever took their daily toll. In the few weeks before their deportation, the able-bodied Jews were taken out to work in various parts of the city. These undertakings often acquired a punitive and

degrading character. On a Sabbath, for example, a group of
Orthodox Jews were given the assignment of destroying the
interiors of the Great Synagogue. While in the ghetto, the
Jews, and especially the formerly well-to-do, were subjected
to humiliating experiences by Christian teachers, civil servants and midwives, who were searching for "hidden" trea-
sures as instructed at a secret meeting of April 26, held in the
City Hall of Munkács ... The deportation of the Jews was
pre-arranged in accordance with the well-established scheme
whereby the local authorities would request the removal of
the Jews 'because of the health and feeding difficulties prevailing in the ghettos ...'

With the formalities settled, and in accordance with the
decision of the "transportation conference" of Vienna, May 4
to 6, the Reich Security Main Office informed the German
Foreign Office of its decision to begin the deportation of
Hungarian Jews on May 15 and to carry it out by means of four
trainloads   daily   through   Carpatho-Ruthenia,   Kassa,
Myszyna, Tarnow and Cracow.

For this purpose, Hungary was divided into six deportation zones: Carpatho-Ruthenia acquired the ominous distinction of being identified as deportation zone I. The deportations from the Hungarian provinces were carried out in four
distinct phases, according to closely detailed schedules. The
first phase involved the deportation of 289,357 Jews from
zone I and zone II (Transylvania) between May 15 and June 7,
1944. The deportations took place under the most horrible
and inhuman conditions. The day before the deportations
began, hospital patients, newborn babies, the blind and deaf,
the mentally disturbed and prison inmates of Jewish origin
were all brought into the ghettos. Immediately before their
transfer to the railroad station, the Jews were again subjected
to a thorough search for valuables. Men and women were
forced to undress in the yard and maltreated in front of their
children.

Upon their arrival in Auschwitz, the Jews of Carpatho-
Ruthenia were "processed" in the now well-known manner.

Most were immediately taken to the gas chambers. Relatively few escaped the Auschwitz inferno, only to be scattered in a variety of concentration camps throughout Nazi-controlled Europe. Of these, very few returned to their native homes at the end of hostilities.

U.S. Rescue Efforts

We, the descendants of those who perished in the Holocaust, have a right, well-nigh a duty, to ask questions which will lead to embarrassing answers. This is particularly true in the case of the Hungarian phase of which we have just read, involving the slaughter of 600,000 Jewish men, women, and children within a few months of 1944. These were the months during which the Allied armies landed on the beaches of Normandy on D-Day, June 6, and when the Russian armies advanced from the east of Europe toward the heart of *Festung Europa* (Fortress Europe). The Hitler regime, which was supposed to have lasted for 1,000 years, was beginning to fall apart after just over 10 years of existence. Yet, in the short period of World War II, it managed to slaughter more than twenty million people of all nationalities, races and religious groups. From the start, the principal target of this onslaught had been the Jews. Even in 1944, a year when the Germans should have used every available resource for fighting the war on the various battlefields, they diverted trains, troops and resources to transport more than half a million Hungarian Jews to Auschwitz and other crematoria. Relevant questions as to why and wherefore have to be asked over and over again, if only to learn what happened, what went wrong. For if we, the survivors and the students of that period, do not learn from past mistakes, similar tragic events may recur in the future in other parts of the world.

Our basic outline follows the findings of Professor Henry Feingold, the historian, who in his article, "The Roosevelt Administration and the effort to save the Jews of Hungary," has raised questions and given answers for us to ponder.[15]

The article points out that, "Until January 1944, the concern of the Roosevelt administration about the Holocaust was minimal and lacked credibility." Lack of understanding within the State Department and restrictive immigration laws prevented any large scale escape of Jews to the United States. Moreover, official United States policy held that Palestine, the natural haven of refuge for Jews, came within the British sphere of interest. And the United States did not want to pressure its ally to open the gates of Palestine for more immigrants. News of the Nazi genocide and "Final Solution" began reaching the State Department in 1942, but was deliberately suppressed. Then, in 1943, reports of the Nazi killings had become so widespread that they created heavy pressure upon the American and British governments to look for a new policy of rescue. Finally, in January 1944, a new agency was created in the United States—the War Refugee Board headed by John Pehle. Its immediate attention was focused on rescuing the three-quarters of a million Jews living in Hungary. We have already seen that this country's independent policies had thus far preserved its Jewish population much to the chagrin of the Germans. Then, when Hitler's armies occupied Hungary in March of 1944, it became apparent that the Nazi deportation policies would soon engulf Hungary. John Pehle succeeded in having President Roosevelt issue an appeal to the Hungarians on March 24, 1944, not to cooperate with the deportations. Pehle also tried to involve the British Government, the International Red Cross and the Vatican, but with little success.

Equal failure accompanied Pehle's efforts to induce the military in Washington to bomb key agency locations and rail junctions leading to Auschwitz. Dread that Budapest might be bombed had led to the countermanding of the deportation order by Admiral Horthy. Pehle sent a letter requesting precision bombing of selected targets, to John J. McCloy, Assistant Secretary of the Army, on June 29, 1944. The latter's reply of July 4 is quoted here because it must be viewed as the attitude of the military, which, in turn, reflects the policy of the Roosevelt administration:

> ... Such an operation (bombing) could be executed only by the diversion of considerable air support essential to the success of our forces now engaged in decisive operations elsewhere and would in any case be of such doubtful efficacy that it would not warrant the use of our resources. There has been considerable opinion to the effect that such an effort, even if practicable, might provoke more vindictive action by the Germans ...

Feingold calls this reply "one of the most tragic documents to come out of the Holocaust" and remarks, "What more vindictive action than Auschwitz was possible, remains the secret of the War Department."

Undaunted by the negative retort of the Washington authorities, Pehle tried to influence neutral countries to increase their diplomatic missions in Hungary, hoping that this would deter the Hungarians from cooperating with the Nazis. One of these neutrals, Raoul Wallenberg of Sweden, succeeded in saving at least 20,000 Jews by issuing them Swedish passports and placing them under the protection of the Swedish Diplomatic Mission. There also were negotiations in which the War Refugee Board, the American Joint Distribution Committee and the Jewish Agency for Palestine were deeply involved. The names of Saly Mayer, the Swiss representative of the Joint, and Roswell McLelland, the representative of the War Refugee Board, must be recorded here for their tireless efforts to save Jews.[16] Mention must also be made if only briefly, of the unsuccessful and controversial scheme to exchange Jews for trucks in which Eichmann and R. Kasztner of the Jewish rescue committee in Budapest, were leading figures. In the end, all of these efforts saved only a limited number of Hungary's Jewry. When the Soviet armies liberated the ghetto of Budapest on January 18, 1945, only 119,000 half-starved and emaciated Jews were found alive out of 762,000 counted on March 19, 1944. Had it not been for the Russian advance, few of these Budapest Jews would have remained alive at all. By December 1944, an extermination factory had been built by the Germans and the Hungarians in Budapest; it was to have started "operations" in January and to finish what Auschwitz had been unable to do. An old market opposite the Academy of Music had been converted into this "Hungarian Auschwitz," very efficiently situated near the ghetto where most of the Jews had been moved from their homes. Fortunately, it never began functioning.[17]

Conditions of the Jews upon the Russians' arrival were extremely bad. The people were sick and without proper medical attention. The little food that was available was high-priced. Inflation was rampant and local resources within the comunity non-existent. The occupying power, namely the Russians, did not distinguish between Hungarian Jews and non-Jews. All were considered Hungarian and therefore enemies. The Hungarian parties continued with their anti-Semitic propaganda calling for a "Budapest free of Jews," and claiming "that four times as many Jews seem to have returned as had been deported." Nadich reports:

> . . . The result of all this among the Jews was confusion and panic. Large numbers of Jews were rushing into the churches for conversion to Christianity, having learned little from the lesson taught by the Nazis. Scores of women had visited the Synagogue in Budapest during the High Holidays of 1945 wearing crosses around their necks and watching carefully before they entered, making certain that no Christian should see them going into a synagogue.

When Dr. Joseph J. Schwartz, Chairman of the European Executive Council of the Joint, visited Hungary in October, he said, "Hungarian Jews were the most tragic on a continent abounding with tragedy."[18] Had it not been for the energetic help of the Joint, many of the survivors would have died. Almost 100,000 men, women and children were fed daily in soup kitchens. More than four million dollars, the highest per capita appropriation in 1945, were spent by the Joint to rescue Hungary's surviving Jewry from starvation and disease.

4.
FROM CONCENTRATION CAMPS TO DISPLACED PERSON CAMPS

U.S Army Meets Survivors

Our story now leads us into Germany proper where we will learn more about the Hungarian Jews that survived the Holocaust. Our statistics tell us that approximately 116,000 returned to Hungary by the end of 1945. Sixty thousand returned to Hungary proper, 40,000 to Northern Transylvania and 16,000 to Subcarpathian-Ruthenia.[1] It would be impossible at this point to try to find out where and under what circumstances all of these Jews were liberated.[2] Were they in concentration camps in Germany, Austria or Poland, and if so, which ones? Or had they been serving in labor companies at the Russian front, liberated by the Red Army and returned to their former homelands with the Czech Army?[3] Were they on forced marches, driven by the SS and rescued by the Allied Armies or had they been living in hiding under false names and identity papers? Whichever it was, each and every human being has his own story to tell, a story so horrible that it can never be told in full. What one can and must attempt is to give the major outlines and perhaps high points of individual experiences, so that they should never be forgotten.

In this attempt, the writer is aided by his own experiences and observations gathered while serving as a U.S. Army Chaplain with the 5th Infantry Division, one of the major units of General Patton's Third Army. A native of

Subcarpathian-Ruthenia, he had been raised and educated in Germany. In the United States since 1938, he was fortunate in being assigned to the European Theater of Operations. He had been anxious to learn abut the fate of his own parents who had been living in Stuttgart, Germany, until the outbreak of the war. He draws on some of the reports written during that period for the following account.

The first report comes from Volary, a little village at the Czech-German border. Our division had advanced across Southern Germany and come upon a group of Jewish girls, survivors from a 1,000-mile, forced march, starting January, 1945 in Silesia and ending in early May 1945.

> This is the story of 1,000 Jewish girls whose ages ranged between 15 and 25. For years they were forced to slave away in Nazi labor camps, supplying the German Army. With the approach of the Russians, they were set to digging tank-traps. In January, they were forced to retreat. Under the whip of the SS men, barely clothed and miserably fed, the women trekked through snow and sleet for over 300 miles. After six weeks, they stopped for a "rest" in a concentration camp, but this place soon became too hot, and again they set out to find new hiding places. Five weeks later, they arrived in Volary, a little Czech village near the German border. Here they stopped, not because the SS men wanted to, but because they could go no further. The Americans had closed the escape gap.

> Out of the 1,000 girls, only 150 were living when they were found. The rest had died from hunger and starvation. Those who couldn't walk were shot by the SS. The survivors looked more like corpses than like girls. Their cheeks were hollow and their bodies were nothing more than bundles of bones; some had gangrene and most could not walk. A few died while being evacuated from a filthy, vermin-ridden barn to a hospital, where medical care given under the supervision of American doctors did wonders for the survivors. After a few days, they already showed signs of recovery.

> This task done, we then turned to exhuming some 50 bodies of girls who had died the week before our arrival. The leaders

of the group were in too great a hurry to bury those who had died on the road. Some of the bodies had been thrown into shallow pits, and were hardly covered with earth; limbs could be seen sticking out of the ground. The Germans themselves had to furnish the labor party to exhume the terrible emaciated bodies. One by one the corpses were disinterred, and, after identification, were laid in coffins. The whole town filed by to see what was done. It was a very hot day and I had anticipated some odor from the decomposed bodies, but there was none; there was no flesh to decompose.

A special plot for the burial was set aside near the regular cemetery. Some people brought flowers. I tried not to be carried away by my emotions, but I felt bitter and sad. I spoke of the guilt of the Germans who, in life and death, had violated the dignity of these young innocent girls whose only crime was to be born as Jews. An American Guard of Honor and many officers and men were present. I spoke English and German to make myself better understood.

The funeral over, I hurried back to the hospital for Sabbath Eve Services in the five wards. We *benshed licht* together, made the *Shehechyanu* benediction for having come out alive, and said the *Shema*, our declaration of faith. I began speaking but my words choked with tears. The girls were crying over their fate and the fate of their families. Where were they: their mothers and fathers, their sisters and brothers, their little children and their friends! I spoke of our mother Rachel who weeps for her children and whose cries are heard in heaven. I tried to fill them with hope and courage.

They had each received a *Mezuzah* and a Prayerbook which made them very happy. I stopped at each bed and shook hands with all of them, blessing them and wishing them a *Guten Shabes*. They could hardly utter words of thanks, but their eyes reflected their innermost feelings.[4]

Our second report deals with the horrible conditions within the camps at the end of the war. The Third U.S. Army area of responsibility included Bavaria and Austria where most of the camps were situated. Criticism had been filtering through, that not enough was being done to improve the lot of the survivors. Being the Senior Jewish Chaplain of Third Army, I was assigned by the staff Chaplain, Colonel O'Neill, to tender a special report on my visits to various camps. The target of the criticism was General Patton himself, who had been a very successful military leader, but was less understanding of civilian needs. It ultimately led to his removal as Commanding General of Third Army by General Eisenhower himself.

SUBJECT: Report of Detached Service in Displaced
            Persons' Camps
TO: Chaplain (Col.) James H. O'Neill
            Hq Third U.S. Army, APO 403, U.S. Army

21 May 1945
Arrived in Linz, Austria at noon.
Contacted Division Chaplain of the 65th Inf. Div. who introduced me to the Officers concerned with the Displaced Persons' problem. Approximately 800 Polish and Hungarian Jews, who had left the Nazi Concentration Camps after the arrival of the Americans, are scattered throughout the city in small groups.
They are running out of food and adequate medical care.
They refuse to return to Nationality Camps, such as Polish or Hungarian, because they had received, in Nazi days, discriminatory treatment.
The anti-Jewish sentiments still persist among many of the DPs.
Met with various leaders of these small groups.

22 May 1945
Searched for a Camp site.
Met Chaplain Golden of the 11th Armored Division, north of the Danube River, who prepared a camp for Polish Jews in his area, capacity 150.
Conferred with American Red Cross and Military government officials.
Miss Christian of the ARC and Captain F.D. Giacome, both of whom promised help.
Obtained passes for Jewish leaders.

23 May 1945

Camp approved in 65th Inf. Div. area near Linz, Austria, capacity 350.

Visited Neubau, 14 kilometers from Linz.

Approximately 10,000 Displaced Persons, mostly Jews.

One hospital (121st Evac) and one Clearing Company have medical supervision and are assisted by 30 Doctors taken from the DP group itself, and by German Medical Officers and men.

The hospital is operating since the 12th of May 1945.

Of late supported by one UNRRA Team.

The average daily death rate is 35, mainly from malnutrition and typhus.

24 May 1945

Spent all day at Neubau, visiting with patients.

Established Dr. Martin Gutman, a Hungarian Rabbi, as the religious leader of the Camp.

25 May 1945

Visited Concentration Camp Mauthausen and sub-Camp Gusen.

These were extermination camps.

They are now under the supervision of the CCB of the 11th Armored Division, and are supported by two Evac Hospitals (130 and 131st).

War Crimes Commission functioning.

Next to the Camp is a stone quarry where the inmates had to work.

Conducted two funeral Services.

Visited both Evac Hospitals.

Visited Camp established by Chaplain Golden, condition excellent.

Meetings with Polish Jewish groups in Linz, Austria.

Established officially accredited leaders of the Polish and the Hungarian Jews, with the American Military Government.

Conducted Sabbath Eve Services at Neubau.

26 May 1945

Procured clothing and shoes for 100 persons for Linz Camp.

26-29 May 1945

Returned to base at Vilshofen, Germany.

30-31 May 1945

Visited DP Camps in Cham, Germany.
Condition of the 500 Jews in the area is satisfactory.
Two DP Camps supervised by the 410th FA Group, APO 403, US Army, supported by the 120th Evac Hospital.
Visit with patients in local civilian hospitals in Cham.

1-2 June 1945

Attended Conference at Army Rear to meet Chief of Chaplains and his party from Washington, D.C.

2-3 June 1945

Visited Dachau, north of Munich, Germany.
Supervised by the 45th Inf. Div. and supported by the 116th and 127th Evac Hospitals which are 7th U.S. Army units.
Camp was liberated over a month ago.
Religious program well organized by Chaplain Robert O. Beck of the 116th Evac Hospital, APO 758, U.S. Army.
At present, 2,400 inmates of Jewish faith.
They were looked after by Chaplains Eichhorn and Braude.
I also heard that a Jewish Chaplain is due to arrive.
A Jewish Information Office has been organized; it is concerned with the inner discipline and welfare of the inmates.
Health: in general improving.
According to a statement made by Dr. L. Goldstein, a civilian Doctor and X-Ray Specialist at the Camp hospital, the Jewish hospital patients are mostly tuberculosis cases.

Recommendations:

1. Civilian Jewish relief agencies be allowed to procure additional food and clothing for the restoration of these Nazi victims to a more normal state of health.

2. Establishment of Jewish Camps wherein those can remain whose disposition at the present is uncertain. For an example—Many Polish Jews do not want to return to Poland.

3. An American Jewish Chaplain be permitted to visit these camps from time to time to provide religious guidance and counsel.

Our third report was sent to Rabbi Philip S. Bernstein, the executive director of the Committee on Army and Navy Religious Activities, National Jewish Welfare Board. This organization was the official link between the War Department and the Jewish Community of America. Two of its functions were to endorse rabbis for service and to supervise Jewish religious programs in the military. This report was written from my new assignment with the First Division, scheduled for occupation duty in Germany:

The 1st U.S. Inf. Div. of which I am the Jewish Chaplain, since June 20, 1945, extends over the area which is commonly known as the Regierungsbezirk Mittel and Ober Franken. It does not contain any specifically Jewish camps, like the ones I helped organize while on detached service with the 3rd Army prior to the above date and of which you received a report, but it contains a number of large cities which, due to the fact that they are railroad centers, attracted a great number of released Jewish people. The cities are Bamberg, Nürnberg, Fürth and Ansbach. My main work has been carried out in Bamberg and Ansbach.

Bamberg: A large east-west traffic stop, it now has approximately 500-600 Jews. The census was possible due to the fact that we were able to issue a bottle of wine to each person for the High Holy Days. A committee is functioning under my supervision and we were able to accredit them, through Military Government officials, with an automobile. I mention this specifically, because transportation is one of the main problems in the organization of active help. The synagogue in Bamberg was destroyed and we set out to establish a suitable hall to be used as a synagogue. This place of worship was dedicated a week prior to Rosh Hashanah.

At the present time we have two projects:

1. To avail ourselves of the maximum amount of temporary

relief. We are mainly dependent upon our own resources, i.e.
collections among the soldiers. (I made an appeal during
Rosh Hashanah which netted approximately one thousand
dollars.) But more than money, the need is for food and
clothing. As for food, I saw a limited amount of *"Vaad
Hatzalah"* packages, which appeared substantial. Then the
committee received some supplies through the International
Red Cross, located in Bayreuth. Looking at these packages,
which are supplemented by shipments from my Boston Serve
a Chaplain Committee, and by packages sent to individual
soldiers and donated to us for distribution, I was filled with
pride in the American people, who make such a great effort in
behalf of the needy in Europe. I have read a great deal concerning the Joint Distribution Committee, but have yet to
meet one of the representatives of this organization. It is
hoped that they maintain closer liaison with the Jewish Chaplains who are in the forefront of this struggle and who, by
their position, are daily approached for help.

2.   The second project is rehabilitation. There are two phases
to this, one being physical rehabilitation and the other spiritual rehabilitation. Physical: Everyone knows that beyond
temporary relief, which will be a continuous problem, lies the
task of rehabilitation of a more permanent nature. In Bamberg
I have tried to obtain the use of former Jewish property and
machinery which would enable a large number of willing
workers to establish themselves. This could also serve as a
preparation and education for all those who are desirous of
going to Palestine and who want to acquire skills needed in
that country. As yet I am unsuccessful in this operation. There
are too many legal technicalities, which unsympathetic officials can quote, in order to defend their lack of action.It is true
that theater directives command preference for Displaced
Persons, but it does not work out this way. Spiritual: At the
present time the main spiritual activity consists of a weekly
religious service held on Saturday, but this will be increased
to include daily services. There is a great demand for textbooks on all Jewish and general subjects. Many are interested
in replenishing the vacuum created by the years of mental
stagnation. Yiddish and Hebrew books are much desired. We

have been fortunate in allocating JWB supplies for their regular and High Holy Day services, but in the long run these supplies will not suffice. The spiritual regeneration of much salvageable human material depends upon the support of these requests.

Ansbach: This city is important because it is the government seat of approximately two million people. From a Jewish point of view it is also important, because it has one of the very few remaining Synagogues in Germany. The influx of the Displaced Personnel to this town is increasing daily. Here, too, we set up a committee and we are trying to give them temporary relief and also trying to find work for them, which has not been very successful.

Remarks on the Displaced Personnel:

The many years of suffering and escaping from the hangman day by day has left deep imprints upon the few survivors. It seems that they haven't yet begun to realize what freedom means. Now they are people without a direction. They refuse to work for the Germans, for whom they have a deep hatred. They are underfed and undernourished and prefer working in an American kitchen for the meals that they can get there. They are resentful and sensitive; in one way they expect too much from the Americans, and on the other hand it is true that whatever we give them is too little to satisfy their needs. UNRRA help is only available to those that are in camps. Yet the majority of the DPs do not wish to return to a camp. They believe, that since they have been freed from the German concentration camps they should not have to continue living in any camp, no matter how beneficial it may be or under whose jurisdiction the camp is operated. Conditions have definitely improved, if you compare the conditions existing in early May and June, 1945. However they are far from being good. It is hard to understand why the Germans are better clothed, fed and housed, and why the Jew is still on the lowest rung of the ladder.

Recommendations:

1.   Field representatives of the JDC contact and work in close relation with the Jewish Chaplains stationed in Germany.

2.   Extend the aid of the UNRRA to DPs living outside of the camps.

3.   Legalize Jewish committees to act as the legal representatives and custodians for all former Jewish property confiscated by the Germans.

14 September 1945
Ansbach, Germany

The Displaced Persons

Upon entering Germany at the end of the war, the Allies found approximately eight million displaced persons of many European nationalities; the tasks facing the Armies were tremendous.[5] In the U.S. Zone of Occupation—Germany was divided into British, French, Russian and U.S. zones—more than four million DPs were handled from May 8 until July 10, 1945. More than two and a half million were repatriated; more than half a million were turned over to the British, French and Russian authorities. Most had been brought in during the war to work for the German war industry; some had come voluntarily. A total of about 50,000 Jews survived in the various concentration camps of Germany and Austria.[6] The first problem was to restore the health of the survivors. The official Army reports indicate that in Buchenwald, for instance, (the first camp to be liberated on April 13, 1945), the average adult weight on liberation was 60 to 80 pounds, the daily ration 600-700 calories and the daily death rate 200 (60-80 executed). The 20,000 survivors were from 31 nationalities. Bergen-Belsen's camp was mostly Jewish; here 13,000 Jews died *after* liberation, mainly as a result of the forced starvation and epidemics.[7] Similar situations existed in other major camps, such as Mauthausen, Dachau and Ebensee. As we have seen from my reports, the U.S. Army—and other Allied Armies as well—placed complete hospital units at these camps to provide medical care. Many military commanders did this spontaneously as an act of

mercy. Few questions were asked as to nationality or religion of the liberated inmates of the camps. All along, the
Allies had been aware of the problem; ever since 1943, they
had made plans to cope with the millions of foreign nationals
who would be found in Germany at the end of the war. They
had established the United Nations Relief and Rehabilitation
Administration (UNRRA) to provide help to stricken countries through their repective governments and to aid the
Allied Armies in the treatment of displaced persons' problems by providing administrative, medical and welfare
teams. But these teams—by May 5, 1945, there were already
100 in the field—were subject to military regulations. Moreover, the most important needs, namely food, clothing and
housing, also were subject to military control.

In the midst of the millions of DPs and their health and
repatriation problems, the special needs of 50,000 Jews scattered throughout Germany did not immediately receive the
attention they deserved. Not all military commanders realized the extent to which the Jews had been singled out for
persecution not only by the Nazis, but also by the many
collaborators in the countries of Eastern Europe. To have
Jews living in camps together with their betrayers—be they
Poles, Ukrainians, Hungarians, Rumanians or others—was to
continue their misery. During April and May, the British and
Americans considered the need to appoint an advisor on
Jewish problems: H.A. Goodman, advisor for Jewish affairs to
the British Ministry of Information, submitted a personal
recommendation to the Control Commission (British Element) in London, urging such an appointment to establish
closer liaison between the military and the Jewish organizations. The British turned this proposal down, but forwarded
it to the Displaced Persons Branch of Allied Headquarters on
April 28. The reply is quoted in full because it has never
before been made public. It also underlines a dramatic
change of military policy, culminating in the directive of
General Eisenhower of August 22, 1945.

SUPREME HEADQUARTERS
ALLIED EXPEDITIONARY FORCE
G-5 Division
Displaced Persons Branch

10 May 1945

SUBJECT: Jewish Displaced Persons.

TO: Control Commission (British Element),
Displaced Persons Branch, Flat 102,
Ashley Gardens, London S.W.1. (Att:
Lt. Col L.W. Charley, O.B.E.)

1.   Reference is made to your memorandum PWDP/58703/14 dated 28 April 1945 on the subject of the appointment of an adviser on Jewish problems in the Control Council and/or SHAEF.

2.   To answer the specific questions you ask:

(1)   *Has the need for such an adviser arisen so far?*

No. The problems of Jewish displaced persons are similar to those of other stateless and displaced persons persecuted by reason of race, religion or political affiliation.

(2)   *Have you any reason to think such a need will arise?*

If special problems arise, voluntary Jewish welfare organizations, under UNRRA supervision, will be available to handle these problems. It is not considered necessary to have a special adviser on the staff.

(3)   *If the need in our view, is likely to arise, do you not agree that he should be provided by UNRRA who will be responsible for just those specific welfare requirements enumerated above?*

In our opinion UNRRA does not need a special Jewish adviser. It does need personnel experienced in handling stateless and related problems. Such personnel will be available to UNRRA by:

    a.   The direct employment by UNRRA of qualified workers.

    b.   The utilization of qualified voluntary agency personnel.

3.   UNRRA is now arranging for the utilization of person-

nel of Jewish welfare organizations and it is believed that this
is sufficient to handle the problems presented.

For the Chief, Displaced Persons Branch:

A.H. Moffitt, Jr.
Colonel, G.S.C.
Executive Officer

This lack of understanding and clearcut policy from
above spotlights the important role played by the military
personnel who were immediately confronted with the refugee problem. Combat officers, doctors in uniform, GIs of all
faiths did their utmost to improve the situation of the Jewish
DPs. The Jewish chaplains in particular rose to the needs of
their less fortunate brethren and helped to restore them with
a spirit of hope. What brought about the basic change in
United States policy was the action of President Truman
himself. On June 22, 1945, he appinted Earl G. Harrison, dean
of the Faculty of Law, University of Pennsylvania, "to inquire
into the conditions and needs of displaced persons in Germany, who may be stateless or non-repatriable, particularly
Jews." Harrison's inspection trip resulted, on August 1, in a
very strong report in which he described the harsh conditions in the camps, adding:

> . . . the first and plainest need of these people is the recogni-
> tion of their status as Jews. Refusal to recognize the Jews as
> such has the effect of closing one's eyes to their former per-
> secution.[8]

Harrison also echoed the feelings of most survivors when he
urged President Truman to help them resettle in Palestine;
this was to be accomplished through the British government's granting of 100,000 immigration certificates. The
President's speedy reaction brought immediate results for
DPs in the U.S. zone. General Eisenhower, himself a fair and
compassionate person, issued the following directive on Au-

gust 22. It is quoted in full[9], because it instantly affected the lives of every Jewish displaced person and set the guidelines for future policy of United States military authorities:

SUBJECT: Special Camps for Stateless and Non-repatriables
TO: Commanding Generals:
Eastern Military District
Western Military District

1.   It is the established policy of this headquarters, that stateless and non-repatriable persons shall be granted the same assistance as United States displaced persons. This includes ex-enemy nationals persecuted because of their race, religion or activities in favor of the United Nations. Persons discharged from concentration camps, if their loyalty to the Allied cause has been determined will receive all of the benefits granted United Nations displaced persons, even if they were originally of enemy origin, such as German and Hungarian Jews, labor leaders or others put into concentration camps because of political activities or racial or religious persecution.

2.   While persons of Jewish faith who desire to be repatriated to the country of which they are nationals, will be treated as citizens of that nationality and placed in the same centers as other displaced persons of that nationality, those Jews who are without nationality or those Soviet citizens who do not desire to return to their country of origin will be treated as stateless and non-repatriable.

3.   In accordance with the policy of this headquarters, such persons will be segregated as rapidly as possible into special assembly centers. Those who are Jews will be cared for in special Jewish centers.

4.   In establishing these special centers, particular attention will be paid to a high standard of accommodation. Wherever necessary, suitable accommodation will be requisitioned from the German population. Military commanders' powers of requisitioning will be fully utilized in order to insure that these persons are accorded priority of treatment · over the German population.

5.   In accordance with the policy of this headquarters,

special UNRRA teams will be requested for these special centers without delay and these teams will be given maximum operating responsibility and all necessary assistance by military commanders.

The Eisenhower order was of the utmost importance for it eliminated a number of flagrant injustices and made improvement in the methods of treatment of Jewish displaced persons. The first paragraph of the order clarified the unhappy situation of Jews who had, before the war, been living in Germany, Austria, Hungary, Rumania, Bulgaria and Italy. Until the issuance of this order they were in an anomalous situation. On the one hand, they had been subjected to the worst kind of persecution by the Germans and their allies; on the other hand, they were regarded as "enemy nationals" by the officers of the Allies. Both logic and justice demanded that they be accorded preferential treatment by the liberators. Yet, since technically they were citizens of enemy countries, not only could they not receive such preferential treatment, but, if anything, they would be given subnormal treatment.

Of course, it was argued that these Jews were no longer citizens of the several enemy countries from which they had been brought to the concentration camps; their respective governments had deprived them, as Jews, of citizenship and its rights. The reply to such an argument always was that such action by the German government and its allied governments was inhumane and discriminatory against the Jews; it therefore, should not be recognized as valid by the Allied Powers. Thus a tragic-comic paradox was created. Because the democratic army of liberation refused to recognize the acts of discrimination by the enemy—by which Jews were deprived of their citizenship in enemy countries—the Jewish victims of the enemy were now to be regarded also as enemies and were, in spite of their weakened condition, to be deprived of all preferential treatment as former concentration camp prisoners!

   This vicious circle had to be broken at some point, and
paragraph one of this notable order broke the circle. It declared in clear language that "ex-enemy nationals persecuted
because of their race, religion or activities in favor of the
United Nations... such as German and Hungarian Jews,
labor leaders or others put into concentration camps...
would be granted the same assistance as United Nations
displaced persons."

   The Truman initiative also led to the establishment of an
Advisor's Office on Jewish Affairs, and the immediate transfer of Major Judah Nadich, the senior Jewish Chaplain in
Europe, from Paris to Frankfurt. His excellent work from
August to October prepared the ground for the first civilian
Advisor, federal judge Simon Rifkind, who held the position
until March 1946. This office, which became the nerve center
for all activities related to DPs, lasted until December 1949,
and was very ably headed by Rabbi Philip S. Bernstein
(March 1946-September 1947), Judge Louis E. Levinthal (August 1947-November 1947), Professor William Haber (January 1948-January 1949), Harry Greenstein (February 1949-
August 1949) and finally, Major Abraham S. Hyman, who
had served as Legal Consultant since 1946.

   None of the camp survivors wanted to remain in Germany. As soon as it was physically possible, they began searching for other members of their families and returning to their
former home countries, only to realize that there was nothing
to come home to. This was particularly the case for survivors
from Subcarpathian Ruthenia, which at war's end had been
annexed by Soviet Russia, becoming a part of the Ukrainian
Soviet Socialist Republic. The bulk of the approximately
15,000 returnees were labor battalion members who had escaped or been liberated by the Red Army. About 8,500 settled
in the western part of Czechoslovakia,[10] and 4,000 went to
France.[11] Some returned to the U.S. zone in Germany where
they formed a part of the displaced persons population[12]
hoping to emigrate soon to permanent places of settlement.

Others remained in their native homes, trying to adjust to life under the Soviets. They were joined by thousands of Jews from other parts of Russia, mainly office workers and technical administrators in industry. Estimates list the number of all Jews by 1971 as more than 13,000.[13] These new settlers who spoke little Yiddish and no Hungarian were not as tradition oriented as the local Jews. Instead, they spoke Russian and had been raised in the atmosphere of secularism. It is no wonder that both Jewish groups, native and Russian, lived far apart from each other, spiritually and culturally. What they developed in common was a growing desire to emigrate to rejoin other members of their families and raise their children in a free environment according to the dictates of their own conscience.[14]

While President Truman was able to improve the situation in the U.S. zone of Germany and Austria, his recommendation that the British admit 100,000 Jews to Palestine fell on deaf ears. The pressure for resettlement in Palestine began to mount in 1946, due largely to the influx of Jews from Poland. These were Polish citizens who had been repatriated by the Soviet Union, but could not find their place in Poland. The influx became expecially heavy after the Kielce pogrom of July 1946, during which 41 Jews were killed. Kielce was an episode reminiscent of medieval pogroms in which Jews had been accused of murdering Christian children in order to use their blood for ritual purposes. That this should have been possible in 1946, a year after the Hitler regime had been destroyed, created a great deal of panic among the Jews of Poland. It showed them that anti-Semitism was still a strong force in the land, a force which the government and the church were unable or unwilling to control. Even before the pogrom, there had been an exodus of Jews from Poland. The figures for May and June were 4,000 and 8,000 respectively, increasing in July to 19,000 and in August to 35,000. This exodus soon raised the number of DPs in the U.S. zone from 50,000 to 150,000, of which 100,000 lived in camps and the

rest in the cities. The newcomers put a heavy strain on housing accommodations and educational facilities. While most
of the people liberated in 1945 were single persons, now
many family units began to arrive. There developed great
uneasiness within the military, which had hoped the DP
problem would decrease instead of the opposite. Added to
their misgivings was the influence of British Foreign Minister Ernest Bevin, who dismissed the new arrivals as "organized Zionist pressure," designed to open the doors of
Palestine. All these pressures made General Joseph T. Mc-
Narney declare on August 6, that "all organized movement of
Jewish refugees will be turned back from the American zones
of Germany and Austria in the future." He added, "The
United States had never adopted a policy for the American
zone being a station en route to Palestine or any other place."
But, once again, compassion combined with political pres-
sure in Washington prevailed, easing the stand of the mili-
tary sufficiently to accept new refugees into the U.S. zone of
Germany and Austria.

These were hectic days and weeks, full of crises and
confrontations, as this writer can attest from personal experience. When the refugees poured in from Poland by way of
Czechoslovakia, they were kept in the U.S. zone of Austria
until all the camps there had been completely filled. Then
they were shipped from Salzburg, Austria, into camps in
Germany. Jewish chaplains were assigned as escort officers
to help with the transport of these frightened souls, scared to
move into the land that had brought death to six million Jews.
Many had heard about "Minchen" (the Yiddish name for
Munich, Germany) as the place where they might be able to
gain news about missing relatives and friends. In Munich,
Jewish life had become more organized, with functioning
committees concerned about helping them in the present and
the future. As a result, Jewish refugees often jumped off the
train when they saw it pass through the city. This trend
became so strong that trains were scheduled to pass through
Munich at night to avoid their seeing it. Still, they kept

asking how far they were from "Minchen," and soon after arriving in their respective camps, they could be seen in the offices of the committees in Munich, searching for answers that often could not be given.

Although the refugees were better cared for in camps, they preferred living in the cities. Having suffered enough from past regimentation, they often rebelled at being brought to yet another camp. This writer vividly recalls the incident of Babenhausen, a camp formerly used by the Germans for prisoners of war. When the more than one thousand DPs involved saw the camp with its barbed wire fences and dilapidated barracks, they refused to leave the train. For three days running, day and night, we tried to use our persuasive powers, hoping to convince them that under the circumstances this was the best the Army could provide. Even General Keyes, Commanding General Third Army, pleaded personally with the people, promising an improvement in the camp facilities. Finally, the bulk of the people agreed to enter the camp provided that the wire fence be removed immediately.

After the influx from Poland a new stream of 20,000 refugees began to arrive from Rumania, along with several thousand from Hungary and Czechoslovakia. Finally, on April 12, 1947, Army authorities closed the camps to further entry. This was indeed a crisis year with the highest number of DPs and the lowest rate of emigration. This was also the year when many tried to reach Palestine "illegally" and were interned by the British on the island of Cyprus: 4,000 Jews on board the ship "Exodus 1947" were forcibly returned to Germany by the British Navy, which intercepted the boat near the shores of Palestine. At long last, the establishment of the State of Israel on May 14, 1948, started a steady flow of DPs, which by December 31, 1950, passed 120,000.

To sum up this period of DP life, the presence of Holocaust survivors in the DP camps exercised great pressure all around and led to the creation of the State of Israel. Thus, in a small measure, the sufferings of the DPs was not entirely in vain.

5. | IN THE UNITED STATES

The war against Germany ended in May 1945, freeing approximately 50,000 Jewish survivors from the concentration camps. It took about one year until some of them were able to reach the shores of the United States. There were a number of reasons for the long time lag between liberation and emigration. First the physical condition of the survivors had to be restored to a passable standard of health before they could start out on the journey across the ocean. Then, many wanted to search for their families in their countries of origin, quests that proved futile most of the time and left the refugees even more depressed than before. Finally, most of the survivors preferred to go to Israel (then called Palestine) and rebuild their lives in the Jewish homeland of old. This is clearly reflected in the figures, which show that between December 15, 1945, and September 15, 1946, a total of 15,000 immigrants arrived in Palestine from the displaced persons camps of whom 9,296 were so-called "illegals," traveling in the boats of the Haganah's secret rescue fleet. The rest held certificates issued by the British Mandatory Government and allocated by the Jewish Agency.[1]

The official immigration statistics on the influx of displaced persons into the United States start on May 1, 1946. By June 30, 1948, a total of 41,379 DPs had arrived, of whom about 27,500 were Jewish. The flow was made possible by a directive from President Truman, dated December 22, 1945, which authorized the use of available quota numbers for natives of Central and Eastern Europe and the Balkans living as DPs in the U.S. zones of Germany and Italy. It further authorized the use of U.S. government transportation to speed the newcomers' arrival. December 22, 1945, however, became cut-off date for these special immigrants. Only those who had been in the DP area prior to the date of the directive were admitted. Since thousands of DPs arrived in the U.S. zone after this date, Congress subsequently passed two laws enabling a total of 250,000 DPs to enter the United States by July 11, 1951; of these 77,500 were Jewish.[2]

There are no accurate statistics as to how many came from Subcarpathian Ruthenia, the primary interest of our study. There were many from this area who wanted to come to the United States because they had relatives in various parts of the country, most of whom were eager to help the remnants of their families adjust to new surroundings. Many relatives belonged to societies called "Landsmanschaften," each of which represented immigrants from a particular community in the old country. Many of these societies had formed early in the 20th century, and their history is part of the saga of Jewish settlement in the United States. The "Landsmanschaften" were tiny islands of ethnic identity in the vast ocean of Jewish immigrants. They provided social and religious programs as well as financial support in cases of need. A major objective was the purchase of cemetery plots, a function that in the old country had been part of the Jewish community's responsibilities. As no central Jewish communal organization existed in the new country, it became imperative that societies assume such caretaker roles. Their other functions included support of synagogues, local welfare institutions and needy people in the old country. With the establishment of the State of Israel they also became very active in its behalf.[3]

It is beyond the scope of this volume to go into the history of the societies representing immigrants from Subcarpathian Ruthenia. In New York, for instance, there are groups which trace their origin to Huszt, Körösmezö, Munkács and Ungvár.[4] Some date back to the turn of the century, growing in numbers with the immigration after World War I and now declining as ties to the old life style wane and acculturation to America takes hold. After World War II, a number of new groups organized and affiliated with the fraternal Zionist organization, Bnai Zion. There are chapters for Beregszász, Bistritz, Munkács, Máramaros-Sziget, Szöllös, Técsö as well as Transylvania.[5]

Our study will concentrate more on the Hasidic groups and certain personalities who originated from Subcarpathian Ruthenia and the surrounding regions. Theirs is a fascinating story which begins with the period after World War II when the United States became the haven for many Hasidic survivors of the Holocaust. Our special attention is drawn to the Satmarer Hasidim and their leader, Rabbi Yoel Teitelbaum.[6] We last read about him upon the demise of his older brother, Chaim Tzvi, who had been the communal rabbi of Sziget until 1926. At that time, Rabbi Teitelbaum, aged 40, a mature leader with a large following of his own, might have succeeded his brother, whose oldest son had barely reached the age of 14. The communal elders, however, preferred the young son, which prompted Rabbi Teitelbaum first to move to the Rumanian community of Carei (Nagy-Károly) and then, in 1934, to Szatmár, in Northern Transylvania, then also a part of Rumania. In 1940, Transylvania was annexed by Hungary, which made Rabbi Teitelbaum as well as all other Jews of this region victims of Hungary's anti-Semitic policies. With the occupation of Hungary by German troops (March 19, 1944) and the start of the deportations to Auschwitz, the Rabbi tried to escape in May across the Hungarian border into Rumania, but was caught, thrown into the Ghetto at Cluj and then deported together with many others to Bergen-Belsen where they remained until December 1944. As a result of financial arrangements with the Nazis carried out by

Rudolf Kasztner[7] with the cooperation of the Jewish Agency
for Palestine, Rabbi Teitelbaum and 1,368 other Jews from
Hungary were then shipped to neutral Switzerland, where
they arrived on December 7, 1944.[8] After a brief stay in
Switzerland, Rabbi Teitelbaum went to Palestine and then, in
1946, to the United States, settling in Williamsburg, a section
of New York City's Borough of Brooklyn.

Rabbi Teitelbaum's arrival signaled the beginning of a
remarkable career, or rather the continuation of one, that had
already shown signs of brilliance in the old country. It is
amazing that Rabbi Teitelbaum managed to overcome the
bitter experiences of the Holocaust and rebuild a large following with a wide ranging chain of religious, educational
and social institutions. Today, thirty-five years after the Rebbe's arrival in the United States, at the age of sixty, a great
deal of material has been published which, coupled with the
personal research and interviews of this writer, provides us
with a fair amount of objective information.[9]

Since the growth of the Satmarer movement was a direct
result of Rabbi Teitelbaum's leadership, it is imperative that
we first sketch the major features of his philosophy. As out-
lined by Lamm there are four major premises:

1. God alone will redeem Israel in the supernatural, miracu-
   lous manner, making His power manifest. Israel will remain passive as history comes to an end without human
   intervention. All Israel must do is submit to the yoke of
   exile, while it waits faithfully and lives in accordance
   with the Divine will, i.e. Torah.

2. There can be no redemption prior to repentance. Even if
   the Messiah were to come before the mass repentance of
   the Jewish people, the actual redemption would be delayed until such collective religious return to God took
   place.

3. It is inconceivable and absurd that God should bring on
   redemption by means of those who deny and hate Him.
   Hence, Zionists and the State of Israel are in effect obsta-

cles to the true redemption because they are a source of secularism.[10]

4. Democracy is valid for non-Jewish political communities only. For Jews, democracy is utterly unacceptable. Only the laws of the Torah, as interpreted by its authorized commentators, are applicable to Jews. The Zionist state, a majority of which is non-religious, and of which even the religious Zionist faction accepts democracy, is untenable and reprehensible.[11]

In reading these statements one can readily see why they must be unacceptable to most of the Jewish people today. But before examining why they are so, it should be stressed that Rabbi Teitelbaum's philosophy, extreme as it was, represents a continuation of a philosophy articulated in the early days of Zionism, about one hundred years ago. Jews have prayed for a rebuilding of Zion ever since the destruction of the Temple, believing that the Exiles' return to the Holy Land would be accomplished by Divine Providence. This belief enabled Jews to adjust in the many countries where they were allowed to reside. They saw their life in them as ultimately only temporary; the spiritual home of the Jew was always Zion, which the Almighty would rebuild in His own good time. While such a religious outlook helped sustain the Jewish people despite all the human misery and political inequality suffered in their places of residence, it no longer sufficed in the 19th century when ideas of human rights began penetrating the Jewish masses of Eastern Europe. More than ever, it was felt that the solution of some of the Jews' problems depended upon organized political action. One of these problems, anti-Semitism, stirred Theodor Herzl (1860-1904), a Jew far removed from a religious concept of Judaism, into organizing a movement that would ultimately change Jewish history. Herzl hoped that the creation of a Jewish state would eliminate anti-Semitism and give Jews the equality denied them in the diaspora.[12] The bulk of Herzl's supporters as well as the movement's leaders after his demise came from the

masses and intelligentsia of Eastern European Jewry; many
were secular in outlook, often rebellious against the rabbinic
leadership of the day, whom they viewed as reactionary and
obstructing progress. Only gradually, in the course of the
20th century, did the more progressive religious leadership
join the forces of Zionism. They hoped that their cooperation
within the movement would imbue the national goals of
Zionism with the religious elements needed to tie it to their
historical and traditional concepts of Judaism. Our own story
has shown us that the rabbinic leadership of Hungary, and
particularly the Hasidic rabbis of communities such as
Munkács, Sziget and Szatmár, produced the most militant
leaders against Zionism before the outbreak of World War II.
There was a genuine fear that Zionism would undermine the
traditional beliefs of the people, leading to a secular kind of
Jewish life.

Rabbi Yoel Teitelbaum had been one of those militant
leaders. He continued in the same vein after coming to the
United States in 1946. However, his extreme position against
Zionism and the state of Israel was not supported by most of
religious Jewry. Even though many of the Hasidic and Orthodox rabbis shared Rabbi Teitelbaum's concern for traditional values, they felt that these could be better realized
within the framework of the state, and not in total opposition
to it. In the light of the Holocaust, in particular, when so
many millions of Jews had been killed just because they were
Jews, the Satmar opposition to a Jewish state became impossible to defend. True, the State of Israel did not represent the
theocracy that Rabbi Teitelbaum would have liked to see. But
this very state, born out of the ashes of the Holocaust and
fought for with the blood of thousands of young men and
women, was providing a home for millions of Jews, one
where they could live in dignity and be respected by other
nations.

Had Rabbi Teitelbaum's attitude and struggle been
merely one of being against something, in this case, Zionism,

a historical reviewer could have found it easy to join those rejecting him and his philosophy. One, however, is forced by the facts to report the other side of the Satmar story, a side based on the very solid accomplishments of Rabbi Teitelbaum and his followers.

If increasing numbers are a sign of success, the Satmarer movement must be considered very successful. Kranzler, in his careful analysis of the Williamsburg Jewish community, vividly describes the impact made upon Jewish life by the Hasidic rebbes.[13] In the early days, there were a number of them, but in the course of events Rabbi Yoel Teitelbaum proved to be the outstanding one. Originally, the bulk of his followers must have come from the two thousand Hungarian Jewish immigrants of the late 1940's. They probably knew of him or had been his admirers in Europe. It was only natural that they should cling to him for guidance amidst the new surroundings of America. It also was natural that these newcomers should want to remain in the Williamsburg area, the home base of the Satmarer Rebbe, even though the neighborhood with its dilapidated housing was not very appealing. Within these limited surroundings, Rabbi Teitelbaum developed a large network of communal institutions, which operated either exclusively under his direction or under the guidance of those who had his confidence. Today the total number of his followers in the New York area is estimated at 50,000.[14] Their private school system, described as the largest in the world,[15] educates approximately 7,000 students, according to Rabbi Hertz Frankel, principal of secular studies in the girls schools. Frankel, who came to the Satmarer movement in the 1950's, told this writer, that the Rebbe was deeply involved in all decision-making processes of education. This is understandable in that "girls' education" and "secular studies" are issues going to the heart of Satmar philosophy. It is well-known that in the very religious circles of old Satmar, the major educational thrust was reserved for boys. The principal objective of education was to teach the boys Torah in order that they might live according to its precepts. Even when secular education became compulsory in Hungary, Hasidic groups tried to get by with the minimum. Formal Jewish studies for girls, particularly on an advanced level, were practically non-existent. As Rubin states:

> Jewish book learning was considered not only unnecessary but actually undesirable for women. The few skills and laws a woman needed to be able to fulfill her role in the home were taught informally by the mother. As for secular education, girls unlike boys, were in most cases permitted to attend the elementary public schools.[16]

Rabbi Teitelbaum's views on education did not change upon coming to America. On the contrary, they became stronger in face of the ever present threat of assimilation. Yet, ways had to be found, and are still being found, to abide by the law of the land, which requires secular education for boys and girls up to the age of 16. At the same time, classes for both could not deviate from the objective of Satmar education, which is life according to strict Jewish law as interpreted by the Rebbe himself. Even a casual observer must admit that the Satmarer educational system has succeeded in upholding its own goals. The boys do not pursue any higher secular education for the sake of a career, and the girls accept the role of homemaker as their ordained status in life. A woman takes pride in having a large family, and her concern for them is her major occupation.

The strength of the community is very much dependent upon living in the same neighborhood. As for ways of earning a living, the men seek positions that do not require a college education, taboo in the eyes of the Satmarer. To this end, they have developed training programs to teach manual skills and technical vocations. They also have their own employment service with listings of thousands of business establishments ready to accept Hasidic workers. Fortunately, the five-day work week in the United States makes strict Sabbath observance easier for the Satmarer as well as other religious Jews who are prepared to undergo economic hardship for the sake of Torah observance.

It is a credit to city, state and federal agencies that they have recognized need and come to the assistance of the Hasidic community. Under the leadership of Rabbi Leopold Lewkowitz, the Opportunity Development Association (ODA) was formed in 1974 to serve the Hasidic community in the New York metropolitan area. It provides business people with technical assistance and help in preparing applications for small business loans, thus far enabling more than 1,000 Hasidim to obtain millions of dollars in loans from various agencies.[17] In 1977, with the help of the U.S. Department of Commerce, ODA prepared a blueprint, "South Williamsburg, a Strategy for Preserving a New York Neighborhood," which contained a number of recommendations concerning housing, employment, commerce, open space, local traffic, environment and community service. Translated into action, these recommendations should prove beneficial to all residents of the district, including the Hispanic as well as the Hasidic community.

While ODA's community efforts are designed principally for Williamsburg, there is also a substantial Satmar presence in the Borough Park Section of Brooklyn, Monsey, New York, and Lakewood, New Jersey. Long before ODA began functioning, Rabbi Teitelbaum felt the need to improve living conditions for his people, at least for those willing and able to leave congested Williamsburg. In 1962, his people bought a 500-acre tract in Mount Olive Township, New York, 35 miles west of Manhattan, where they hoped to build houses. This plan did not succeed, however, due to local zoning restrictions.[18]

A second attempt in the mid-1970's was more successful, leading to the establishment of Kiryat Yoel (City of Yoel [Teitelbaum]) in Monroe, a township in Orange County, New

York, approximately 50 miles north of New York City. Here, too, a great deal of opposition involved Jews and non-Jews alike. It was based on a lack of understanding about Hasidim generally, and the Satmar movement in particular. The Hasidim's outward appearance—beard, curly earlocks, black garb and white shirt—immediately projected a different life style. Their strict observance of Jewish law also set them apart from the general Jewish community, which sometimes became defensive about its own less rigid concept of Judaism versus that of the Hasidim. As some of the Satmar families began moving into the area in 1974, open opposition soon developed among some neighbors who felt that their own property rights were infringed upon. The local newspaper printed an article, "Satmar's arrival in Monroe no cause for alarm."[19] But the media's attempt to allay the community's fears did not succeed as the conflict continued all through 1975 and 1976. At issue was the development of Monfield Homes, near Monroe, where more than 500 Satmarer had moved into 25 houses and 80 garden apartments. The town board accused the Hasidim of having converted 18 single-family houses into multiple-family units, even though the area was restricted to single-family dwelling units. The town demanded that the zoning violation be corrected, and ordered work stopped in another part of the development where it feared more conversions. The leaders of the Satmar Hasidim disputed the allegations, insisting that they were within the law. Their family units were large, they said, often including not only parents but also married children and their families. Accusing the town of inhospitable behavior, they contended that there was lack of understanding for their way of life.[20] The battle moved into state and federal courts, but finally better judgment prevailed and the Hasidim's petition to incorporate the Monfield development into a self-governed village was approved by the Town Supervisor of Monroe in December 1976.

The 320-acre village became Kiryat Yoel, now occupied

by several hundred families.[21] A grateful community built a magnificent synagogue with a seating capacity of several thousand to accommodate the many faithful who would visit the Satmarer Rebbe on the High Holidays and other festive occasions. It reflected their devotion to the Rebbe and their ability to raise huge sums among his followers in all parts of the world. These contributions, amounting to millions of dollars, sustain a vast network of schools and Yeshivot in the United States and Israel. They also cover the social and welfare needs of the community, which tries to take care of its own. One of its newer activities in the last few years has been RAV TOV, a committee to aid newcomers.[22] The program deals principally with new immigrants from Russia. Its objective is to help Russian Jews adjust to America while teaching them the traditional Jewish way of life.[23] Despite taking on these responsibilities, the Satmarer Hasidim as a whole are not a wealthy community. There are many impoverished families with large numbers of children. For example, during the recession in 1974, the unemployment rate in the Hasidic community increased from the usual six percent to 20 percent.[24] Accordingly, the community has a very big loan society with interest-free loans to those in need.

While the Satmarer have succeeded in becoming the largest Hasidic group in the New York area, it must be stated that their public image has not always been very good. This fact, which has not escaped the attention of observers of the scene, is readily acknowledged by the Satmarer themselves.[25] Their anti-Zionist attitude set them apart from almost every other segment of the Jewish people, particularly in the United States. Here, where the support for the State of Israel so deeply occupies the heart and mind of the American Jew, a different point of view, no matter how sincerely advanced, causes immediate rejection. The Satmar ideology is featured in a Yiddish weekly, Der Yid (The Jew). While many Orthodox groups in the United States and Israel sympathize with some of the religious issues raised by this paper, they

reject the methods with which the Satmarer pursue their
point of view. When it leads to burning of Israeli flags or
fighting in the streets among Hasidim of the various sects, a
committed Jew must feel great distress. One such outburst
led to street fighting on the Sabbath of April 9, 1977, which
was also the last day of Passover. The occasion was a march of
the Lubavitcher Hasidim from Crown Heights to Williamsburg. To see bearded Jews fighting each other, with police
trying to separate them, was certainly a sorry spectacle. But
painful as it was, it reflects (in a very crude and despicable
manner), some of the differences between these two strongest
Hasidic groups. It is important that we gain a better understanding of these differences.

Rabbi Bernard Weinberger of Williamsburg's Young Israel congregation has been a close observer and participant in
communal affairs since 1955, and his reports reflect the life
within the various Jewish groups.[26] His article "Satmar and
Lubavitch: The Dynamics of Disagreement" was written in
the wake of the "Passover fracas" between the two groups.[27]
It tries to analyze the various divisions among the Hasidim,
the values that they have in common and the differences that
often keep them apart. He sees a contrast in style between
Lubavitch and Satmar Hasidim, which reflects the surroundings in which both have lived. Lubavitch, a community in
Russia, had to struggle with Czarist and Communist regimes
in order to survive. In particular, the Communist challenge to
the spiritual life of Lubavitch required boldness and brazen-
ness in opposition. Still, it was not as strong a physical threat
to life as that of the Nazis, which often demanded shrewdness
and bribery, at least from those who managed to survive. But
even before the Nazi threat to the very life of all Jews, the
Hungarian Hasidic leadership, including the Satmarer, was
very much concerned about "the future deterioration" of
spiritual values within the Hasidic community; it moved into
an ultra-traditional corner, resisting any kind of innovation
or association with other religious parties. Satmar's concept

of *Hasidut* begins with the self-effacing premise that it is no match for the Hasidut of the original disciples of the Baal Shem Tov, the founder of the Hasidic movement; neither the leaders nor the followers of today are worthy heirs of the pious men of generations ago. "Yes," Weinberger says, "they have retained the traditions and forms of the Hasidim of old, but they recognize that the passion and fervor, the purity and piety of their grandparents is beyond them." The Satmarer Rebbe himself has been the strongest advocate of self-knowledge, seeking every means at his disposal to dissuade his thousands of followers from attributing to him the mystical standing of the *Tzaddik* of old. This in spite of the fact that by every conceivable standard he qualified as a Tzaddik in the classical Hasidic tradition of the term. He enjoyed a pedigree that linked him with all of the greatest Tzaddikim. By erudition, scholarship and piety, he was eminently qualified to assume the role of the Tzaddik. Yet, no one has done more to discourage that role than he himself.

One might add that the conceptual differences between Satmar and Lubavitch are very much evident in the practical programs by which they pursue their goals of strengthening Judaism. Satmar is exclusive and defensive; Lubavitch is outgoing and more attractive to the average Hasidic and non-Hasidic Jew. Satmar has become strong in America because it is very strict in its demands of personal behavior; Lubavitch has become influential because it reaches out to all Jews, trying to bring them back to an understanding and observance of Jewish law. The reach of the Lubavitcher Rebbe is worldwide. Whenever the present incumbent, Rabbi Menachem Mendel Schneerson, delivers a discourse from his headquarters at 770 Eastern Parkway in Brooklyn, New York, it is transmitted by an intricate telephone hook-up to his followers in 27 countries, including Israel.[28] Near universities in the United States, there are now 77 Lubavitch CHABAD centers that serve as religious oases for many students.[29] Then there are the Lubavitch Mitzvah Mobiles, buses

used by followers who distribute ritual objects to Jewish
passersby, encouraging them to greater observance of tradition.

As for the Satmar movement whose phenomenal growth
was very much the work of Rabbi Yoel Teitelbaum, his demise on August 19, 1979 at the age of 93 was a great blow to
his thousands of followers. His scholarship and leadership
had been so outstanding that it will be very difficult for his
successor to live up to his role. However, the momentum
created by Rabbi Yoel will no doubt inspire the faithful to
follow in his path.

Another Hasidic group that must be mentioned here
because of the role it played historically in the geographical
areas of our study is the Vishnitzer Hasidim whose rebbes
and followers touched the lives of Jews in Hungary,
Czechoslovakia and Rumania.[30] Its strongest personality in
the late 19th and 20th century was Rabbi Israel Hager (1860-
1936) whose views are reflected in some of the stories in Part
Two of this book.

The Vishnitzer life style is characterized by an emphasis
on love of God, love of Torah and love of Israel. A prolific
family, it had many branches throughout the old country,
most of them destroyed during the Holocaust. Fortunately,
one leader, Rabbi Chaim Meir Hager (1888-1971), managed to
reach Israel, where he established a large community with
many educational and social institutions in Bne Brak. Normally, a firstborn son succeeds in the position of Rebbe upon
the demise of his father. In the case of the Vishnitzer, however, there are now two Rebbes, one Moses Joshua (born
1916), who is in Bne Brak and his brother, Mordechai (born
1922), who first organized his followers in Williamsburg.
Then, in 1965, he decided to take some of his Hasidim to
nearby Monsey in Rockland County, New York, where they
set up a community away from the hustle and bustle of the
crowded city. There is a close relationship between the two
brothers, with mutual support in their many educational

activities in Israel and throughout the world. Through marriages of his daughters, the older brother became the father-in-law of some very important Hasidic rabbis.[31] All of these alliances reflect a desire of the few Hasidic dynasties that survived the Holocaust to maintain their special standing among themselves and within the Hasidic community.

Finally, there are two more Hasidic dynasties trying to carry on in the tradition of their illustrious forefathers. Rabbi Jacob Joseph Weiss, head of the Spinker Hasidim, divides his time between Israel and New York. In both places there are many religious and educational institutions maintained by his large following.[32] Rabbi Moishe L. Rabinovitch, grandson of Rabbi Chaim Elazar Spira of Munkács, also has developed a very active religious and educational program in Brooklyn's Boro Park.[33]

The geographical identity of those Jews from the northeastern counties of Hungary who moved to the United States after World War II is fast disappearing. Now they go under the general name of "Hungarian Jews" or Hasidim who follow a certain rebbe. The second generation, born in the United States, speaks Yiddish rather than Hungarian, increasingly with working knowledge of English. Characteristic of the Orthodox and Hasidic elements is the near absence of a generation gap among immigrants and their children, the effect being an uninterrupted standard of spiritual values. Families stay close together providing future protection against less desirable outside influences. Clinging tenaciously to tradition, they are not only strong within themselves, but also exert a great influence upon others sympathetic to religious values.

Of course, no one can predict how long this attempt at insulation or isolation in special communities will remain successful. Most members make their living within cities and are bound to be influenced by the mores of their American surroundings. Moreover, how long can Hasidim do without higher education for their children in a society where college education has become a very important factor for economic advancement? What will happen to the high birthrate at a time of increasing cost of living? While the strong family structure reduces the rate of divorce, too few data exist to determine to what extent, if any, there has been an erosion of the Hasidic life style.

OUTSTANDING PERSONALITIES

Lest it appear that only Hasidim are concerned with traditional values, this writer selected three from a large number of personalities who have dedicated their lives to Jewish survival. The first is a rabbi's rabbi, the second a scholar's scholar and the third has become the spokesman for the six million Jews who perished in the Holocaust.

Rabbi Isaac Klein

The first is Rabbi Isaac Klein (1905-1979), who arrived in the United States in 1921 from the little village of Palánka, Hungary, where he received his early Talmudic training. He continued at the Isaac Elchanan Yeshivah in New York, but found he wanted more than Yeshivah training. This "more" he found in the person of Professor Louis Ginzberg (1873-1953) of the Jewish Theological Seminary of America who combined the Talmudic scholarship of the East European Yeshivot with the critical-historical approach of the western universities.[34] Ginzberg ordained Rabbi Klein in 1937 with the special degree of *Hattarat Hora'ah* (Permission to Judge), which is given only in the case of special erudition in Talmudic literature. As he had already been in the active rabbinate for several years Rabbi Klein was fully aware of the realities of Jewish life in America. His concern is expressed in these words:

At the moment of speaking, I thought to myself, what is really going to happen to Judaism? Do we have to resign ourselves to this superficial and sham institutionalism that is called "religious" in America? And even if we should not yield, can individuals defy the majority and cloister themselves in so that they be not touched by these cross-currents of banalities. I always pray to God that at least in my own life, I may make our good and pure and sacred traditional religion a source of strength and beauty, with the further hope that perhaps the day will come when religion will again be a force in the daily life of humanity.[35]

Klein's first published work, "The Ten Commandments in a Changing World," also reflects the major concern of his rabbinic career. It appeared in 1944 when he already was serving as a chaplain in the U.S. Army and was ready for overseas assignment in Europe. He had volunteered for such duty, although he could easily have stayed out of the war being in his late thirties and the father of three young children. But this was characteristic of Isaac Klein. He always wanted to be where he could do the most good for his people and humanity. After return from four years of active duty, Klein's days were filled with being a busy rabbi, a relentless scholar and a teacher of rabbis and other students. In 1948, he was awarded a Ph.D. from Harvard University.[36] Then, in the late 1940's he took leave once more from his congregational duties to serve with the temporary rank of Brigadier General, as an Advisor on Jewish Religious Affairs to the U.S. High Commissioner of Germany. In the 1950's, he devoted much time to helping the Hungarian refugees pouring into the United States and visiting military installations to advise chaplains on their duties. In 1958, Klein's colleagues elected him president of the Rabbinical Assembly for whose committee on Laws and Standards he had written many responsa. His basic objective was to show that Jewish law can and must be made viable in all areas of life. Thus, in 1959, when the chancellor of the Seminary, Dr. Louis Finkelstein, invited him to lecture in New York on "Laws and Standards of Religious Observance," he accepted, even though this meant frequent absences from his Buffalo home and congregation.

Klein saw in this invitation an endorsement of his efforts and an opportunity to guide young rabbinical students in their future careers. In preparing his discourses, Klein availed himself of the latest scientific research, tying it to the findings of recognized legal authorities. This is how he introduced his *Guide to Jewish Religious Practice* published after his demise:

> All through my preparation of this code, I was conscious of the underlying philosophy of the Conservative Movement and its unique approach to Jewish law, which takes into consideration the historical and sociological factors, both past and present, operating in the development of the Halacha. When Rabbi Moses Isserles wrote his glosses on the Shulchan Aruch, he insisted on the authority of the scholars of Eastern Europe and on the validity of the practices (minhagim) that obtained in the East European communities, even when these were at variance with the laws laid down by Rabbi Joseph Caro.
>
> In like manner, in preparing this work I have insisted on the authority of our Conservative scholars and on the validity of the practices of our Conservative congregations . . .Isserles added the practices that obtained in Eastern Europe of his era, and I have added the practices that obtain in the present-day Conservative Synagogue. The code I have prepared, therefore, will serve as a guide for those congregations that are affiliated with the United Synagogue and the World Council of Synagogues, as well as for individuals in accord with their principles.

Klein's monumental efforts will undoubtedly serve as an important bridge from the past into the future.

Rabbi David Weiss Halivni

The choice of our second personality is as fitting as our first. Fortunately, Professor Halivni is still very much with us, which brings his past achievements much closer and makes his future efforts more intimate. He was born in 1927 in Polyana Kobelecky, a small village in the Carpathian Mountains, and grew up in Sziget, in the house of his maternal grandfather, the eminent scholar, Rabbi Isaiah Weiss. While still very young, Professor Halivni impressed his teachers with his brilliant mind, which prompted Rabbi Gross of the Yeshivah of Sziget to ordain him at the age of fifteen. Two years later, the young rabbi and his entire family were deported to Auschwitz. He alone survived, suffering extreme hardship in various concentration camps.

In February 1947, Professor Halivni arrived in the United States. Anxious to resume his Talmudic studies he first entered Brooklyn's Yeshiva Chaim Berlin. At the same time and by special arrangement, he attended Brooklyn College and New York University, from which institutions he obtained degrees in philosophy. During the 1950's, the greatest Talmudic scholar in New York City, Professor Saul Lieberman of the Jewish Theological Seminary, attracted Halivni to continuing his studies at the Seminary. He calls Lieberman "his Teacher, a Giant of Torah and Science who stood by him at the crossroads of his life and brought him into the gates of true Torah."[37] After ordination in 1957 and a Ph.D. in 1958, Professor Halivni remained at the Seminary first as an instructor and later as a full professor of Talmud. Since 1968, he also has been an adjunct professor of religion at Columbia University.

What then is so exciting about Halivni and wherein lies his major contribution to Judaism? The answer is at once simple and involved: simple, because he deals with a primary body of Jewish literature, and involved because to fully understand him requires vast erudition that only a few achieve in their lifetimes. The following is a modest attempt to bring the reader closer to Professor Halivni's thinking.

We must bear in mind that the Jewish people possess two principal sources of tradition. First there is the Bible, which goes back to Mount Sinai and before; then there is the oral tradition in explanation of the written word. For hundreds of

years, religious leaders passed on this oral tradition by word
of mouth, handing it down thus to succeeding generations.
Approximately 1,800 years ago, the oral tradition was put
into writing, which became the Talmud, an accumulation of
thousands of pages dealing with every aspect of Jewish life.
The Talmud and the Bible formed the two anchors by which
Jews have held fast throughout their long and turbulent history. Mastery of the Bible and Talmud with all their commentaries and supercommentaries became the ultimate goal
of Jewish education. This mastery was more than an intellectual exercise, it was a guarantee for Jewish survival. If
we were just to say that Professor Halivni has achieved this
mastery in an unparalleled manner, we could admire him,
but would not fully comprehend his special contribution to
Judaism. This contribution became very evident after his first
volume of *Meqorot u'Mesorot* (Sources and Traditions) appeared in 1968, followed by a second volume in 1975, with a
third soon to be published. The complete *Meqorot u'Mesorot*
is to be a nine-volume commentary on the entire Talmud.
Professor Halivni subtitles the study "Source Critical Commentary," offering the following definition of his approach:
"Source Criticism seeks to differentiate between the original
statements as they were enunciated by their authors and the
forms they took as a consequence of being orally transmitted,
that is, between the sources and their later traditions. It is not
to be confused with the kind of analysis which merely traces
the historical sources of a given passage without judging
whether or not the passage faithfully reflects the sources.
Source Criticism claims that the transmission of the Talmud
was not, and perhaps could not have been, verbatim, and that
the text became altered in transmission, with the result that
many statements in the Talmud have not come down in their
original form. Instead, what survives is the form assumed in
the last phrase of transmissional development. While such a
study is pertinent to most ancient texts, it is particularly
relevant to the Talmud, which primarily consists of quota-
tions and their interpretations."[38]

This statement, technical as it may sound, is recorded here in full with a definite purpose: to whet the reader's appetite to delve into the world of Talmud as Professor Halivni sees it. Mind you, Professor Halivni is not the first one in modern times to follow the road of source criticism. In the 19th century H.M. Pineles (1805-1870) in Galicia, and in the 20th century J.N. Epstein (1879-1950) at the Hebrew University of Jerusalem, both pioneered in this same field. It does not come as a surprise, however, that Professor Halivni had a difficult time at the beginning of his scholarly work, for there were those from the Yeshivah world who resented his association with the Seminary, which to their minds made any of his findings suspect from the start. They saw in his teachings a challenge to their deep belief that both Bible and Talmud are of Divine origin. It is not difficult to understand that a professor of Halivni's background, with his personal piety and strict adherence to all minutiae of Jewish tradition, must be very sensitive to such reservations. He has tried to meet them head on, showing that criticism and Divine Revelation are compatible with each other.[39] Moreover, Professor Halivni says that acceptance of criticism need not involve changes in Halachic practice, a process that may not always go hand in hand with historical reality.

In a more recent article, Professor Halivni also deals with the academically trained Talmudic scholars and their methods of study. He finds definite weakness in their close adherence to the text, equating scholarship with variants and parallel sources. Such scholarship often remains on the surface, he contends, preventing it from a deeper understanding of the text itself.[40] Rather, Professor Halivni advocates his own method, designed to separate the original from what accrued later, the "Sources from the Traditions," by constantly asking who said exactly what and how—and how much, if anything at all, was subsequently altered through either transmissional or redactional changes.

Today, Professor Halivni has achieved the unique distinction of being called a "scholar's scholar." His books are a "must" in the academic curriculum of Talmudic studies both here in the United States and in Israel, where Professor Halivni often lectures at Bar Ilan University in Ramat Gan.[41] He was featured in a very comprehensive article in *The New York Times*, publicity to which he does not object because it brings Talmudic thought to the widest attention.[42] It also promotes interest in the general academic community. All along, Professor Halivni has felt that the undergraduate curriculum of our universities should include courses on Rabbinic Judaism, which covers the period from the third century B.C.E. until the third century C.E.; surely the Rabbinic writings of these five hundred years have contributed greatly to the development of Western civilization. Professor Halivni's proposal to spread knowledge of this period led to a government grant, enabling the Jewish Theological Seminary to organize summer institutes for academics in 1978 and 1979. More than twenty carefully selected, college teachers of all faiths and from universities throughout the land gathered each summer for intensive studies of Rabbinic writings under the guidance of Seminary faculty members. Admittedly this is a small beginning, but certainly a move in the right direction. To Professor Halivni personally, it must bring a great sense of satisfaction to see his life's ambition gradually realized: that is, to deepen the knowledge of Talmud in all circles and to carry on the tradition of learning, thereby contributing to the survival of the Jewish people.

Elie Wiesel

It is only logical and, in a sense, climactic that Elie Wiesel is the last of our three personalities. For whatever has been written thus far can serve as a bridge toward better understanding of an individual who, in the relatively short span of twenty years, has become one of the best-known thinkers and writers on the national and international scene. Much that has been said about David Weiss Halivni and his early history may be applied to Elie Wiesel. About the same age, they are close friends and both call Sziget their home community, having shared there an intensive Hasidic background of piety and learning. Wiesel too was greatly influenced by his grandfather, Reb David Feig, a devout Hasid, who introduced his young grandson into the world of Hasidism. Wiesel writes movingly about his grandfather, by whose name he is known in Vishnitzer Hasidic circles even today. They call him Dodye Feig's grandson. Since much of Wiesel's writing is autobiographical, it is well to hear what he has to say about his grandfather: "The stories that I most like to tell are the ones I heard from my grandfather. I owe him my love of tradition, my passion for the Jewish people and its unfortunate children. And he, who never read a novel, is a presence in my novels. My old men often bear his features, sing the way he did and, like him, disarm melancholy with the magic of words."[43]

Young Wiesel, along with his fellow Jews in Sziget, suffered the fate of deportation to Auschwitz, where all of his family were killed, leaving him miraculously a lone survivor in a world where there was no going back to old surroundings. By chance, he ended up in Paris after the war, studying philosophy at the Sorbonne and earning his living as a newspaperman writing on the current scene for French, Hebrew and Yiddish papers.[44] His stay in France left him with a deep love for the French language, in which he writes his major works. During his early years in France, Wiesel wrote nothing about his concentration camp experiences. After his liberation from Buchenwald in 1945, he had made a vow to keep silent for ten years about his personal life. In the course of his work as a journalist, however, he became acquainted in 1954 with Francois Mauriac, the respected French Catholic writer, who urged him to write about this intensely painful period in his life. Wiesel's first work, La Nuit, appeared in a French translation from the Yiddish in 1953; an English version, "Night," followed in 1960 with a very eloquent foreword by Mauriac himself.

Almost like a gushing fountain, words began flowing from Wiesel's pen, creating a sequence of remarkable books on the period of the Holocaust.[45] They were accompanied by a multitude of appearances, lectures and interviews, which quickly propelled him into becoming the principal spokesman for the survivors of the concentration camps. Even more, Wiesel developed into a much sought after professor of the Nazi era, all this despite his conviction that one cannot "teach" the Holocaust; one can only teach what one fully understands. To quote, "No, I do not understand. And if I write, it is to warn the reader that he will not understand either. 'You will not understand, you will never understand' were the words heard everywhere during the reign of night. I can only echo them. You, who never lived under a sky of blood, will never know what it was like. Even if you read all the books ever written, even if you listen to all the testimonies ever given, you will remain on this side of the wall, you will view the agony and death of a people from afar, through the screen of a memory that is not your own."[46] A little later, Wiesel states that he writes because he *has* to. Quoting Goethe, he says, "When man, in his grief, falls silent, then God gives him the strength to sing of his sorrows. He must do so to wrench the victims from oblivion and to help the dead to vanquish death."

This approach, dirgelike and yet more compelling than a dirge, gives Wiesel's work a mysterious dimension. He does not speak for himself, but for the millions who have no voice and for whose experiences he testifies like a witness. He is driven to write and to teach, uttering words that God puts into his mouth. He must speak out no matter how painful it may be. Thus it should come as no surprise that Wiesel spoke out in April 1978 against the television drama, "Holocaust." For no matter how good the intentions of the producers, the experiences of this era are an "ultimate event, an ultimate mystery, which can never be comprehended nor transmitted. Only those who were there know what is was; the others will never know."[47]

Wiesel himself is objective enough to realize that the story of the Holocaust must be told, although he claims not to have the answer as to how. His voice becomes almost drowned out by those who point to the millions of viewers all over the world for whom this television series provided a first introduction to the horrors of the Nazi period. Wiesel rejects the film because he, "the witness, cannot recognize himself in it." The Holocaust must be remembered, but not as a show.

Wiesel's writings not only have affected Jews very deeply, but also many, many non-Jews. A recent survey found leading Protestant and Catholic personalities in agreement that he has opened their eyes to the implications of the Holocaust and to the need for reshaping Christian thinking and living. They were determined to attack the sources of evil that made the Holocaust possible and to prevent a recurrence in the future. They appreciated Wiesel's statement that "the sincere Christian knows that what died in Auschwitz was not the Jewish people but Christianity."[48] This statement, painful as it may be, is accepted because it comes from a sincere Wiesel who also says, "I feel closer to certain Christians as long as they do not try to convert me to their faith—than to certain Jews."[49] And again, "I felt closer to Pope John XXIII and to Francois Mauriac than to self-hating Jews. I have more in common with an authentic and tolerant Christian than with a Jew who is neither authentic nor tolerant." Wiesel does not want to hurt anyone, but as the sincere witness he has a duty to ask the following questions: "How is one to explain that neither Hitler nor Himmler was ever excommunicated by the Church? That Pope Pius XII never thought it necessary, not to say indispensable, to condemn [concentration camps, such as] Auschwitz and Treblinka? That among the S.S. a large proportion were believers who remained faithful to their Christian ties to the end? That there were killers who went to confession between massacres? And that they all came from Christian families and had received a Christian education. Wiesel speaks frankly, but not because he wants to divide people. His aim is to bring all peoples together, Buddhists, Arabs, Europeans and Americans. Seeing himself as a witness, he asks, "What is a witness?" And he answers, "A witness is a link, a link between the event and the other person who has not participated in it. A witness is a link between past and present, between man and man, and man and God. Being a witness I would like to be that link between the Arabs and the Jews, and the Jews and the Christians, and the Jews among themselves."[50]

In November 1978 President Carter named Elie Wiesel as the chairman of a commission composed of distinguished Americans of all faiths.[51] Its task was to recommend ways for the United States to honor the six million Jewish victims of the Holocaust. Ten months later, after extensive deliberations and travels to sites in Germany, Poland and Russia followed by a visit to Israel, the commission handed its report to the President. Its recommendations included the building in Washington, D.C., of a memorial museum that would become a federal institution. One of its functions would be to show, through films and pictorial accounts, the existence and culture of Europe's Jews before and during World War II. The commission wisely observed, "Although the Jews were Hitler's primary victims, they were not the only people to suffer for their religious and political convictions." Thus, it proposed that the museum should also have displays on Hungarian, Poles, Russians, Gypsies and others who were murdered by the Nazis. This raised the total from six to eleven millions who would be honored on special days of remembrance to be included in the national calendar. Finally, the commission called for the development of an educational foundation to support studies on the effects of the Holocaust.[52]

President Carter, upon receiving the commission's recommendations from Chairman Elie Wiesel, promised to do everything in his power to carry them out. "The American people," he said, "must forge an unshakable oath with all civilized people that never again will the world look the other way, or fail to act in time to prevent the terrible crimes of genocide. We have not had a constant center which could be visible to all Americans to be reminded of our omissions of the past and to have the memory of this horrible event in our minds to prevent the recurrence of such an action anywhere in the world."

Let us hope that Elie Wiesel and all the world will soon see the fulfillment of these words.

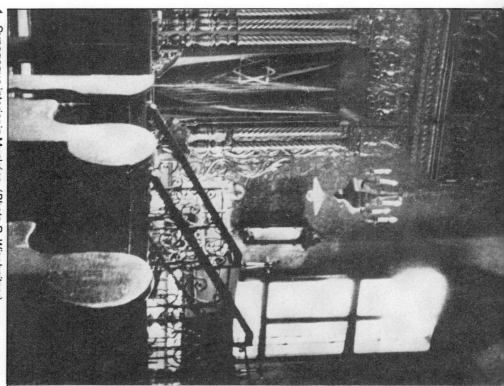

1. Synagogue interior in Munkács. (Photo R. Wischnitzer)

2. Jews in front of the Munkács City Hall. (Photo R. Vishniak)

NOTES

1. The major works on Jews in Hungary and Subcarpathian Ruthenia used throughout this book are listed by their keywords as follows:
   a. *Karpatorus: Encyclopaedia of the Jewish Diaspora* Vol. VII, Karpatorus ed. Yehuda Erez (Jerusalem: Encyclopaedia of the Jewish Diaspora Co, Ltd., 1959).
   b. *Studies: Hungarian-Jewish Studies* Vol. 1-3, ed. Randolph L. Braham (New York: World Federation of Hungarian Jews, 1966-1973).
   c. *Czechoslovakia: The Jews of Czechoslovakia*, Vol. I & II (Philadelphia: The Jewish Publication Society of America; New York: Society for the History of Czechoslovak Jews, 1968-1971).
   d. *Magocsi:* Paul Robert Magocsi, *The Shaping of a National Identity, Subcarpathian Rus', 1848-1948*, (Cambridge: Harvard University Press, 1978).
2. Raphael Mahler, *A History of Modern Jewry* (London: Vallentine, Mitchell, 1971) p. 314 ff.
3. A. Sas, "Die wirtschaftlichen und sozialen Verhaeltnisse der Juden auf dem Dominium Munkács-Szentmiklos im XVIII Jahrhundert," *Juedisches Archiv*, Wien 1928-29, Jahrgang 2, Heft 1-7.
4. Mordechai Schutzman, "Kolomea, Ir ve-Em be-Hasidut," *Sefer Zikaron le-Kehilat Kolomea ve-ha-Sevivah*, ed. D. Noy and M. Schutzman (Tel Aviv: Irgun Yotzei Kolomea, 72) p. 50. Compare: D. Ben-Amos and J.R. Mintz trans. and ed., *In Praise of the Baal Shem Tov (Shivchei ha-Besht)* (Bloomington: Indiana University Press, 1970) p. 211.
5. Dov Noy, "Agadat ha-Besht be-Harey ha-Karpatim," *Mahanayim* (Tel Aviv: Zahal, 1960) p. 66 ff.

6 .Yaffa Eliach, "The Russian Dissenting Sects and Their Influence on Israel Baal Shem Tov," *Proceedings of the American Academy for Jewish Research*, Vol. XXXVI (New York: American Academy for Jewish Research, 1968) p. 57 ff.

7. Gershom Sholem, "The Neutralization of the Messianic Element in Early Hasidism," *The Messianic Idea in Judaism* (New York: Schocken Books, 1971) p. 362; Bernard D. Weinryb, "Reappraisal in Jewish History," *Salo Wittmayer Baron*, Jubilee Volume, English Section, Vol. II (Jerusalem: American Academy for Jewish Research, 1974) p. 939 ff.

8. Raphael Patai, *The Jewish Mind*, (New York: Scribner, 1977) p. 217.

9. Samuel Hakohen Weingarten, "Munkács," *Arim ve-Imahot be-Yisrael*, Vol. I ed. Y.L. Fishman, (Jerusalem: Mosad Harav Kook, 1946) p. 345 ff.

10. For an introduction to his life, see: S. Ehrman, "Moses Sofer," *Jewish Leaders (1750-1940)*, ed. Leo Jung (New York: Bloch Publishing Company, 1953) p. 117 ff.

11. Chatam Sofer, *She-elot u-Teshuvot*, Orach Chaim No 12 (Pressburg 1855).

12. *Takanot Tamchin de'Orayta*, (Munkács 1895).

13. Aaron Wertheim, *Halachot ve-Halichot be-Chasidut*, (Jerusalem: Mosad Harav Kook, 1960) p.17.

14. For a detailed analysis, see: Nathaniel Katzburg, "The Jewish Congress of Hungary 1868-1869," *Studies*, Vol. I, p. 1 ff.

15. Chaim Sofer, *Machane Chaim*, Orach Chaim, Vol. 3 (Jerusalem 1970).

16. For general information, see: Yehuda Spiegel, "Ungvár," *Arim ve-Imahot be-Yisrael*, Vol. IV, ed. Y.L. Maimon (Jerusalem: Mosad Harav Kook, 1950) p. 5 ff.

17. See: Shimon Reinharz, "Rabbi Shlomo Ganzfried," *Karpatorus*, p. 391 ff.

18. See: Leopold Greenwald, *Matzevet Kodesh*, (New York: Hadar Linotyping & Publishing Co, 1952). A detailed history of Sziget still remains to be written. A great deal of information can be found in the handwritten Record of the Burial Society (pinkas Chevrah Kadisha) deposited in the Archives of the Jewish Theological Seminary of America, New York. Its 181 leaves, in Yiddish and Hebrew, cover the wide-ranging activities of this important Sziget society from 1884 to 1922.,

19. Greenwald, *op.cit.* p. 10. For information on Schlesinger, see: Tzvi Zehavi, *Me-ha-Chatam Sofer ve-ad Herzl*, (Jerusalem: Ha-Sifriya ha-tzionit, 1965), p. 2 ff.

20. *Ibid.*, p. 56. The arguments of the Orthodox community were published in *Milchemet Mitzva*, Sziget, 1886 and those of the Sephardic communty in *Ohev Mishpat*, Lemberg, 1887.

21. I am indebted to Dr. Hillel Danzig of Tel Aviv for details about the life of his late father. See also: Shlomo Wiesel, "Mein ersht begegnis mit (my first meeting with) Rabbi Dr. Samuel Danzig," *Máramaros-Sziget*, (Tel Aviv: Irgun Máramarossziget be-Israel, September 1961).

22. Unfortunately, my search in the Joint Archives at New York, 1978, failed to uncover this memorandum.

23. On the role of the Badchan, see: E. Lifshutz, "Merrymakers and Jesters among Jews," *YIVO Annual of Jewish Social Science*, Vol. VII (New York: YIVO, 1952) p. 43 ff.

24. This date is based on a copy, seen by this writer, in the library of the Hebrew University at Jerusalem.

25. Published posthumously as: Hirsch Leib Gottlieb, *Lider fun mein Leben*, (Satmar, Romania: J. Wieder's Buchdruckerei, 1933) p. V ff. It was introduced as the first volume of Gottlieb's works and contains approximately 100 pages of his poems and stories, of which "A Crazy Law Suit" and "Seven Rules for Cardplaying" are included in this book.

26. For an evaluation, see: M. Gorali, "Hirsch Leib Gottlieb, Humorist and Folk Singer," *Proceedings of the Fourth World Congress of Jewish Studies* (Jerusalem: World Union of Jewish Studies, 1968) p. 361 ff.

27. For further information on Centers of Learning and their Leaders in Subcarpathian Ruthenia and Máramaros, see: Abraham Fuchs, *Hungarian Yeshivot, From Grandeur to Holocaust*, (Hebrew) (Jerusalem 1978) p. 461 ff.

28. See: Herbert Weiner, *9½ Mystics* (New York: Holt, Rinehart and Winston, 1969) p. 206 ff. and Eliezer Steinman, *Be-er ha-Chasidut be-Artzot Galicia ve-Hungaria*, Vol. 9, (Tel Aviv: Kneset, no date) p. 329 ff.

CHAPTER 2

1. Ernö László, "Hungary's Jewry, A Demographic Overview 1918-1945," *Studies*, Vol. II, p. 139 ff.
2. On the variety of geographical names, see Magocsi, p. 277 ff. This writer mostly uses Hungarian names since they reflect the language spoken by the Jews of the region. Corresponding geographical terms are listed in the glossary.
3. *Ibid.* p.13.
4. István Végházi, "The role of Jewry in the economic life of Hungary," *Studies*, Vol. II, p. 70 ff.
5. See: Solomon Poll, "The Role of Yiddish in American Ultra-Orthodox and Hassidic Communities," *YIVO Annual of Jewish Social Science*, Vol. XIII, (New York: YIVO 1965), p. 125 ff. On the special linguistic traits of Yiddish as spoken in Subcarpathian Ruthenia, see: Uriel Weinreich, "Western Traits in Transcarpathian Yiddish," *For Max Weinreich On His 70th Birthday*, (The Hague: Mouton 1964), p. 245 ff.
6. Magocsi, p. 95.
7. Isaac Klein, "I remember Palankeh," *Buffalo Jewish Review*, (September 29, 1978) p. A22.
8. Weingarten, *op. cit.*, p. 362.
9. .Yehuda Bauer, *My Brother's Keeper, A History of the American Joint Distribution Committee 1929-1939*, (Philadelphia: Jewish Publication Society 1974), p. 6 ff.
10. This organization spent $100 Million for European relief under President Hoover. The Joint contributed $3.3 Million; in return, its staff was authorized to undertake aid missions for Jews in Eastern Europe as officials of ARA.
11. Moshe Usosskin, *Struggle for Survival*, (Jerusalem: Academic Press 1975), p. 131. While conditions in Transylvania, the former Hungarian province, were also very bad, Rumania as a whole had more food supplies than Czechoslovakia.
12. For biographical information, see: Magocsi, p. 335 f.
13. Aryeh Sole, "Subcarpathian Ruthenia," *Czechoslovakia*, Vol. I, p. 125 ff.
14. *Ibid.*, p. 129 ff.
15. For more information, see: Aharon Rabinowicz, "The Jewish Minority," *Czechoslovakia*, Vol. I, p. 155 ff. and "The Jewish Party," *ibid.*, Vol. II, p. 253 ff.

16. Gertrude Hirschler, "The History of Agudath Israel in Slovakia," *ibid.*, Vol. II, p. 162 f.
17. Hugo Stransky, "The Religious Life in Slovakia and Subcarpathian Ruthenia," *ibid.*, Vol. II, p. 358; also Weingarten, *Karpatorus*, p. 225 f.
18. Magocsi, p. 136. On the Jewish problems in education, see: Aryeh Sole, "Modern Hebrew Education in Subcarpathian Ruthenia," *Czechoslovakia*, Vol. II, p. 411 ff. Sole provided this writer with additional information in an interview at Natanya, Israel, in June 1978.
19. For sketches on his life, see: *Karpatorus*, p. 533-556.
20. Joint Archives, New York; he also received a letter of praise from Rabbi Meir Berlin, the World Mizrachi leader in Jerusalem, who had visited the school in the same year. Rabbi Berlin's praise was tempered by the observation that the school's religious program could be improved.
21. *Festschrift des Hebraeischen Gymnasiums in Mukacevo*, (Mukacevo: 1932). It contains messages in Czech, Ruthenian, German and Hebrew.
22. Beskid's message is printed in Ruthenian and Czech, reflecting his dual role as a Czech official and a champion of Ruthenian autonomy. See also: Magocsi, p. 187.
23. *Czechoslovakia*, Vol. I, p. 152 f.; see also: Livia Rothkirchen, "Deep-Rooted Yet Alien: Some Aspects of the History of the Jews in Subcarpathian Ruthenia," *Yad Vashem Studies*, Vol. XII, (Jerusalem: Yad Vashem 1977), p. 147 ff.
24. Spiegel, *op.cit.*, p. 43 ff.
25. Sole, *op.cit.*, p. 132. Rothkirchen, op.cit. p. 166 f. points to the increased anti-Semitism due to the influence of German National Socialism and that of the White Russians and Ukrainians who had found refuge in Subcarpathian Ruthenia.
26. Rabinowicz, "The Jewish Party," *Czechoslovakia*, Vol. II, p. 302.
27. Gustave Fleischmann, "Religious Life and Organizations," *ibid*, Vol. I, p.300.
28. After World War I Sziget became part of Rumania and as such removed from Rabbi Spira's immediate authority. Being so close to life across the border, however, it often was influenced by his views.

29. For this internal struggle, see: *Kitve Kodesh*, (Munkács: 1928). This volume, published by the Bet Din of Munkács, lists more than 100 rabbis in support of Spira.
30. Rabinowicz, *op. cit.*, p. 297.
31. *Tzava'a* (Testament) of Rabbi Chaim Elazar Spira, (Munkács: 1937). An official biography of the Rabbi, *Sefer Toldot Rabbenu* was published by D. Kahane, (Munkács: 1937). It was reissued by Rabbi Spira's grandson, Rabbi Tzvi Nathan David Rabinovich, in Brooklyn, N.Y., in 1968.
32. Based on personal knowledge, Samuel Weingarten described Rabbi Spira to this writer as a charming personality, visited by people from all walks of life. Dov Dinur, another Israeli historian, formerly from Ungvár, added that the relatively small number of immigrants to Palestine, prior to World War II, was due more to British restrictions than to Rabbi Spira's anti-Zionist views.
33. For more information, see: Armin H. Friedmann, *Major Aspects of Yeshiva Education in Hungary*, (Ph.D. Dissertation, Yeshiva University, New York, 1971) and Shlomo Rozman, *Rashe Golat Israel*, Vol. I, (New York: 1975).
34. In 1924, 796,056 Jews lived in enlarged Rumania which was approximately 5 per cent of the total population: 230,000 in the Old Kingdom, 238,000 in Bessarabia, 128,056 in the Bukovina and 200,000 in Transylvania. See "Rumania," *Encyclopaedia Judaica*, Vol. 14, (Jerusalem: The Macmillan Company, 1972) p. 397 f.
35. Archives of the Joint, New York City.
36. Fuchs, *op. cit.*, p. 543 and Rozman, *op. cit.*, p. 30.
37. Israel Rubin, *Satmar, An Island in the City*, (Chicago: Quadrangle Books, 1972), p. 34 ff.
38. Ibid. p. 37 f.
39. The Agudath Israel organization of Germany and its rabbis had already accepted secular education as part of rabbinic training. This still was opposed by the Orthodox and, even more so, the Hasidic rabbis of Hungary.
40. Friedmann, op. cit., p. 281. During the 1930's three sons of Rabbi Israel Hager included vocational training in their own Yeshivot. They were Rabbis Menachem Mendel of Vishva, Lazar of Vishnitz and Baruch of Seret; see *Matzevet Kodesh*, p. 81.

41. Basch, *op.cit.*, p. 93.
42. David Lazar, "Irgunim u-Mosadot be-Sighet," *Máramaros-sziget*, (September 1967), p. 14.
43. For a concise evaluation see: N. Katzburg, "Le-shitato ha-toranit ve-ha-leumit shel ha-Rav M.S. Glasner," *Memorial Volume for the Jews of Cluj-Koloszvár*, ed. M. Carmilly-Weinberger (New York: 1970), p. 48 ff.
44. Rabbi Greenwald, like many of his fellow Jews in Hungary during the White Terror, was accused of being a Communist, beaten up and thrown into prison for several days. At another time he was attacked by soldiers while standing at the railroad station of Bucharest, Rumania. Information courtesy of Ernest, son of Rabbi Greenwald. For further details on his life and work see: article "Greenwald," *Encyclopaedia Judaica*, Vol. 7, p. 912 and Marc Lee Raphael, *Jews and Judaism in a Midwestern Community*, (Columbus, Ohio: Ohio Historical Society, 1979), p. 262 ff.
45. I am indebted to Naphtali Ben-Menachem's widow for some of these details.
46. Naphtali Ben-Menachem, *Mi-sifrut Israel be-Hungaria*, (Jerusalem: Kiryat Sefer, 1958), p. 100 ff.
47. Basch, *op. cit.*, p. 213.
48. Shlomo Bikel, "Der Szigeter Sholom Aleichem," *Máramaros-sziget*, (July 1962).

CHAPTER 3

1. Kurt R. Grossmann, "Refugees to and from Czechoslovakia," *Czechoslovakia*, Vol. II, p. 565 ff; see also: Fini Brada, "Emigration to Palestine," *ibid.*, p. 589 ff.
2. This had also been the hope of my parents of blessed memory. My father, Joshua Dicker, was born in 1884 in Körösmezö, county Máramaros. My mother, Sara Spindel, was born in 1892 in Dora, Galicia, about 25 miles to the north. Married in 1912, they lived for a short while in my father's town, where I was born in 1914. With the outbreak of World War I, in the same year, my father was drafted into the Hungarian army while my mother fled with her own family to Stuttgart, Germany, where

they had relatives. At the end of World War I in 1918 my father joined them. By now his home town had become a part of Czechoslovakia, which made all of his family Czech citizens. When in 1939 Hungary annexed his county, my parents became stateless. In 1941, they were among the first ones to be deported from Stuttgart to a concentration camp in Lithuania where they perished shortly thereafter.

3. Rabinowicz, "The Jewish Party," *op. cit.*, p. 308; for statements of May 15, 1938 and September 30, 1938 see: *ibid.*, p. 312 and p. 317 f.

4. For Carpatho-Ukraine's internal development see: Magocsi, p. 237 ff. I interviewed Julian Revay, Carpatho-Ukraine's last Prime Minister, in New York, on March 27, 1979. At that time he recalled the liberal attitude of his government towards the Jews. His sudden death soon afterwards prevented him from answering all my questions in detail.

5. Rothkirchen, *op. cit.*, p. 171 f.

6 According to the 1910 census, Hungary's population amounted to 20,886,487 persons, of whom 932,458 (4.64 per cent) were Jewish. The 1921 census lists 7,990,200, of whom 473,355 (5.92 per cent) were Jewish. Erno László, "Hungary's Jewry," *Studies*, Vol. II, p. 138 and 142; see also: Joseph Rothschild, *East Central Europe between the two World Wars*, (Seattle: University of Washington Press, 1977), p. 5 ff.

7. Randolph L. Braham, *The Hungarian Labor Service System*, (Boulder, Colorado: East European Quarterly, 1977), p. 5 ff.

8. This day on which the Vienna Award was finalized gave to Hungary the northern part of Transylvania and to Rumania the southern part with approximately 40,000 Jews. Béla Vágó, "The Destruction of the Jews of Transylvania," *Studies*, Vol. I, p. 178.

9. Bernard Klein, "Hungarian Policies and the Jewish Question in the Inter-War Period," *Jewish Social Studies*, (April 1966) Vol. XXVIII, No. 2, p. 81.

10. Braham, *op. cit.*, p. 29. One of the escapees was Rabbi Baruch Rabinowicz, son-in-law and successor of Rabbi Chaim Elazar Spira of Munkács. See also: Rothkirchen, *op. cit.*, p. 170.

11. Nathaniel Katzburg, "Hungarian Jewry in Modern Times," *Studies*, Vol. I, p. 161.

12. Braham, *op. cit.*, p. 32 ff.
13. Béla Vágó, "Germany and the Jewish Policy of the Kállay Government," *Studies*, Vol. II, p. 183 ff.
14. The gruesome story follows the research of Randolph L. Braham, "The Destruction of the Jews of Carpatho-Ruthenia," *Studies*, Vol. I, p. 223 ff. and Béla Vágó, "The Destruction of the Jews of Transylvania," *Studies*, Vol. I, p. 171 ff. Compare also Gerald Reitlinger, *The Final Solution*, (London, Vallentine, Mitchell, 1968) p. 412 f.
15. *Studies*, Vol. II, p. 211 ff.; see also: David S. Wyman, "Why Auschwitz Was Never Bombed," *Commentary*, (May 1978) Vol. LXV, No. 5, p. 37 ff.
16. See also: Herbert Agar, *The Saving Remnant*, (New York: Viking Press, 1960), p. 156 ff.
17. This is based on Rabbi George Vida's visit to Budapest in October 1945, while on duty as a United States Army Chaplain in Germany. Judah Nadich, *Eisenhower and the Jews*, (New York: Twayne Publishers, 1953), p. 249 ff.
18. "*So they may live again,*" *Annual (1945) Report of the American Joint Distribution Committee*, (New York: 1946), p. 19.

CHAPTER 4

1. See Appendix-Statistics.
2. Jacob Robinson, *And the Crooked Shall be Made Straight*, (New York: Macmillan, 1965), p. 269. "The record shows that the Hungarian Jews, who were selected for labor at Auschwitz, were dispersed to no less than 386 different camps and factories, including the Krupp factory."
3. On the struggle of Czech Jews against the Nazis through service with General Svoboda see: Erich Kulka, *Jews in Svoboda's Army in the Soviet Union*, (Hebrew), (Jerusalem: Hebrew University Press, 1977).
4. *Rabbis in Uniform*, ed. Louis Barish, (New York: J. David, 1962), p. 109. One of the survivors, Gerda Weissman Klein, wrote a moving account of her experiences in *All But My Life*, (New York: Hill and Wang, 1957). In her dedication, she includes the men of the United States 5th Infantry Division, which had liberated her group. One of the officers in charge had been Lt. Kurt Klein, who later became her husband.

5. Chaim Hoffman, "Displaced Persons," *Encyclopaedia Judaica*, Vol. 6, p. 75. Hoffman headed the Jewish Agency for Palestine in Germany after World War II.

6. For detailed information see: Yehuda Bauer, *Flight and Rescue: Brichah*, (New York: Random House, 1970); Kurt R. Grossmann, *The Jewish DP Problem*, (New York: World Jewish Congress, 1951); Herman Dicker, "The US Army and Jewish Displaced Persons," *Chicago Jewish Forum*, (Summer 1961), Vol. XIX, No. 4, p. 290 ff.

7. Bauer, *ibid.*, p. 46. Many of the emaciated survivors could not digest the food available immediately after liberation and died from "overeating."

8. Professor Yehuda Bauer, a specialist of this period, describes Harrison's report as exaggerated, inaccurate and most unfair to the United States Army. Not only did the report accuse the army of cruel and inhuman treatment of Jewish survivors, but it compared the American soldier with the Nazi SS. See: "The Holocaust and the Struggle of the Yishuv as Factors in the Establishment of the State of Israel," *Holocaust and Rebirth*, (Jerusalem: Yad Vashem, 1974), p. 125.

9. Nadich, *op. cit.*, p. 43.

10. This region known as Sudetenland, had more housing available due to the departure of its German population.

11. Braham, "Jews of Carpatho-Ruthenia," *Studies*, Vol. I, p. 233.

12. Dora and Zalman Deblinger, two of my surviving cousins, were in this group. By accident we met in Heidelberg, where I served as an army chaplain. Soon afterwards they entered the United States.

13. "Subcarpathian Ruthenia," *Encyclopaedia Judaica*, Vol. 16, p. 472.

14. Relatives of mine from Jasina joined their family in Israel in 1978 for the same reason.

CHAPTER 5

1. Grossmann, *op.cit.*, p. 23.
2. *Ibid.*, p. 26.
3. For a listing of "landsmanschaften," see: *Di Yidishe Landsmanschaften fun New York*, ed. J. L. Perez Schreiber Parvin, (New York: Work Progress Administration, 1938); for further literature see: Irving Howe, *The World of Our Fathers*, (New York: Harcourt Brace Yovanovich, 1976), p. 689.
4. This listing is undoubtedly incomplete; some of the names of yet other old communities appear on the religious institutions throughout Williamsburg and Boro Park.
5. Information courtesy of Ervin Roth of Bnai Zion, New York.
6. Although Szatmár is not actually within the geographical perimeter of the Carpathian Mountains, the Satmarer Rebbe, Rabbi Yoel Teitelbaum, was a native of Sziget and closely identified with the way of life in the region.
7. Kasztner's activities were aired before the Jerusalem District Court in 1955, where Judge Benjamin Levy found him guilty of cooperation with the Nazis. In 1958 the Israel Supreme Court cleared Kasztner of this verdict, but he had been shot to death on March 3, 1957. See article "Kasztner", *Encyclopaedia Judaica*, Vol. 10, p. 814 ff.
8. The date corresponds to the 21st of the Hebrew month of Kislev, which subsequently became a day of rejoicing for the Satmar Hasidim. It is an ironic twist of history that the anti-Zionist rabbi should have been rescued by the Zionist Kasztner.
9. This writer enjoyed the cooperation of several important functionaries of the Satmar movement, this despite their general reluctance to talk to outsiders. He also benefited from a lengthy interview with Professor Israel Rubin, the sociologist, whose detailed study of Satmar was carried out with the approval of Rabbi Teitelbaum himself. Material on Satmar may be found among the following authors: George Kranzler, *Williamsburg: A Jewish Community in Transition*, (New York: Feldheim, 1961). Solomon Poll, *The Hasidic Community of Williamsburg*, (New York: Free Press of Glencoe, 1962). Norman Lamm, "The Ideology of the Neturei Karta, According to the Satmar

Version," *Tradition*, (Fall 1971), Vol. XII, No. 2, p. 38 ff. Israel Rubin, *Satmar, An Island in the City*, (Chicago: Quadrangle Books, 1972). Seymour Siegel, "Satmar in New York," *Jewish Spectator*, (Winter 1979) p. 20 ff.

10. Lamm, *op. cit.*, p. 46: "The Satmarer thus implicitly and un-compromisingly rejects the well known view of Rabbi Kook (1864-1935) [the former Chief Rabbi of Palestine] that the irreligious by virtue of their zeal and sacrifice for national goals, are unconscious agents of the Divine redemption."

11. Lamm, himself an Orthodox rabbi and now president of Yeshiva University, uses as his sources the following writings of Rabbi Teitelbaum: *Va-Yoel Moshe*, (Brooklyn: Jerusalem Publishing Company, 1959) and *Kunteres al ha-Geulah ve-al ha-Temurah*, (Brooklyn: Sender Deutsch Publishing Company, 1967).

12. For the relationship between Zionism and Anti-Semitism see: Jacob Katz, "Zionism vs. Anti-Semitism," *Commentary* (April 1979), Vol LXVII, No. 4, p. 46 ff.

13. Kranzler, *op. cit.*, p. 102 ff., divides the settlement of Williamsburg into three phases. Phase I, until 1938, reflects the old-type Orthodox Jews; Phase II, until 1948, features principally the Polish-Galician immigrant; Phase III, 1948-1954, is characterized by an influx of 3,000 refugees, two thirds Hungarian Hasidim and one third Polish Hasidim.

14. See: *A Coat of Many Colors, Jewish Subcommunities in the United States*, ed. Abraham D. Lavender, (Westport: Greenwood Press, 1977), p. 14. The 50,000 figure for Satmar and 35,000 given for Lubavitch could not be verified.

15. Stephen Isaacs, "Hasidism in Brooklyn," *ibid.*, p. 101.

16. Rubin, *op. cit.*, p. 137.

17. See: ODA's publication *Today*, (Summer 1978), Vol. III, No. 1.

18. A similar and more successful attempt is the Hasidic community of New Square in Rockland County, New York, approximately 40 miles from Manhattan. The Skvirer Hasidim under their Rebbe, Joseph Twersky, established in 1957 a community, which became incorporated in 1961. For details see: Harry Steinberg, "New Square," Lavender, *op. cit.*, p. 195 ff. The Vishnitzer Hasidim have their own community in Monsey, N.Y.

19. Israel Rubin, *Times Herald Record*, Sunday, December 22, 1974.
20. *The New York Times*, October 17, 1976, p. 53.
21. According to telephone information received by this writer from Mr. Braver, town clerk of Kiryat Yoel, there were as of March 14, 1979, 250 families in the community with 100 more expected in 1980.
22. The Committee has been certified by the Advisory Committee on Voluntary Foreign Aid, Agency for International Development, Department of State, Washington, D.C. Its Chairman, Rabbi Hertz Frankel, assured this writer that it was not the committee's intent to divert Jews from immigrating to Israel. He said, Rabbi Teitelbaum urged its formation upon hearing that some Russian Jews, waiting in Italy, had been offered help by non-Jewish organizations. He was afraid such aid would lead to their conversion.
23. Specially illustrated teaching guides have been printed in three languages — Russian, Hebrew and Yiddish — to teach the newcomers prayers and blessings.
24. Emanuel Perlmutter, "Hasidic Sect Hurt by Unemployment," *The New York Times*, December 26, 1974, p. 41.
25. In addition to Kranzler, Poll and Rubin see also: Jerome R. Mintz, *Legends of the Hasidim*, (Chicago: The University of Chicago Press, 1968) p. 147 ff. and "Brooklyn's Hasidim," *Natural History* (January, 1977), p. 47 ff.
26. "Confessions of an Orthodox Rabbi or a Tale of Three Bridges," *Jewish Life*, Vol. I, No. 1, (Fall 1975), p. 15 ff. and "The Growing Rate of Divorce in Orthodox Jewish Life," *ibid.* Vol. I, No. 3 (Spring 1976), p. 9 ff.
27. *Ibid.*, Vol. II, No. 2-3 (Fall-Winter 1977-78), p. 55 ff.
28. For a warm portrait of the Rebbe see: Irving Spiegel, "The Rebbe: In His Torah There is Room for All Jews," Lavender, *op. cit.*, p. 202 ff.
29. *The New York Times*, March 4, 1979, p. 43. The term *Chabad* is an acronym of three Hebrew words: *Chochma* (wisdom), *Bina* (understanding) and *Daat* (knowledge). They reflect the philosophy of the Lubavitcher movement.
30. The Vishnitzer dynasty traces its lineage to Rabbi Jacob Kopel of Kolomea, a disciple of the Besht, who served as his Hazzan.

For further details see: Yitzchak Alfasi, *Tiferet she-be-mal-chut*, (Tel Aviv: Ariel, 1961) and Neil Rosenstein, *The Un-broken Chain*, (New York: Shengold Publishers, 1976). Much of the information on the movement in the United States was kindly furnished by Rabbi Isachar Gelbman, an official of the organization.

31. According to Rosenstein, *op. cit.*, p. 525 ff., Moshe Joshua's oldest daughter married Rabbi Isachar Dov Rokeach, the Bel-zer Rebbe, who resides in Israel. A second daughter is the wife of Rabbi David Twersky, leader of the Hasidic community of New Square in Rockland County, New York. A third daughter is married to Rabbi Aaron Teitelbaum, whose father, Rabbi Moshe Teitelbaum, became head of the Satmarer movement after the demise of his uncle, Rabbi Yoel, in 1979.

32. Fuchs, *op. cit.*, p. 514.

33. *Ibid.*, p. 506. This writer once tried to elicit some of Rabbi Rabinovich's views on Rabbi Yoel Teitelbaum's anti-Zionist philosophy. His only comment was: "He learned from us," hinting at the anti-Zionist position of his maternal grand-father, Rabbi Chaim Elazar Spira of Munkács.

34. Isaac Klein, *A Guide to Jewish Religious Practice*, (New York: Jewish Theological Seminary of America, 1979) p. 27. For more on Ginzberg see: Louis Finkelstein, "Louis Ginzberg," *American Jewish Yearbook*, Vol. 56 (New York: American Jewish Committee, 1955), p. 573 ff.

35. This statement, written in February 1938, was kindly fur-nished by Mrs. Miriam Shapiro, Klein's second daughter.

36. His dissertation was a translation and commentary on Mai-monides' Code: *The Book of Acquisition* (Sefer Kinyan), which in 1951 was published as Book XII of the Yale Judaica Series. In 1972, Klein's translation, *"The Book of Women"*, appeared as Book IV of the same series, and in 1979, Book VII, *The Book of Agriculture*.

37. David Weiss Halivni, *Meqorot Umesorot*, (Tel Aviv: Dvir, 1968) p. 6.

38. *Ibid.*, p. 729; previously published, *Encyclopedia Britannica*, Vol. XXI (1967) p. 645, article: "Talmud" Source Criticism.

39. "Revelation and *Zimzum*" *Judaism*, Vol. XXI, (No. 2, 1972), p. 205 f. *Zimzum*, a cabbalistic term, means "Withdrawal." The concept is that God sometimes deliberately withdraws from the world permitting man to follow his own inclinations.

40. "Contemporary Methods of the Study of the Talmud," *Journal of Jewish Studies*, Vol. XXX, No. 2, (Autumn 1979), p. 192 ff.

41. Professor Jacob Neusner of Brown University leans heavily on Halivni. See: *The Formation of the Babylonian Talmud*, (Leiden: E. J. Brill, 1970, in which Neusner's students analyze source chapters of Halivni's writings. Compare also Neusner's *A History of the Mishnaic Law of Purities*, Tohorot, Part XII, (Leiden: E. J. Brill, 1976), Preface, p. IX, which is dedicated to Halivni.

42. Israel Schenker, "A Life in the Talmud," *The New York Times Magazine*, (September 11, 1977) p. 44 ff.

43. From an unpublished interview conducted by Rabbi William Berkowitz, November 27, 1976, kindly furnished this writer. See also: "Dodye Feig," in Wiesel's *A Jew Today*, (New York: Random House, 1978), p. 65 ff.

44. *Elie Wiesel, A Bibliography*, comp. Molly Abramowitz, (Metuchen, N.J.: Scarecrow Press, 1974), p. 3 ff.

45. Irving Abrahamson, "Elie Wiesel: A Selected Bibliography," *Confronting the Holocaust: The Impact of Elie Wiesel*, ed. A. H. Rosenfeld and I. Greenberg, (Bloomington, Indiana University Press, 1978), p. 207 ff.

46. *Ibid.*, p. 203.

47. "Trivializing the Holocaust," *The New York Times*, (April 16, 1978), Section 2, p. 11 f.

48. *Responses to Elie Wiesel*, ed. Harry James Cargas, (New York: Persea Books, 1978).

49. *A Jew Today*, op. cit., p. 11 f.

50. *Responses to Elie Wiesel*, op. cit., p. 157.

51. *Daily News Bulletin*, Jewish Telegraphic Agency, (New York, November 10, 1978).

52. Seth S. King, "Museum Urged as Holocaust Memorial," *The New York Times*, (September 28, 1979) p. 14.

3. Main Street, Bustina. (*Photo R. Vishniak*)

4. Father and son in an Ungvár courtyard. (*Photo R. Vishniak*)

6. Title page of *Tamchin Deorayta*, Munkács, 1895.

5. Title page of *Kitzur Shulchan Aruch*, Ungvár, 1864.

7. Rabbi Chaim Elazar Spira, center, in Karlsbad.

8. The last Rabbi of Munkács with his disciples. (*Photo R. Vishniak*)

A *cheder* somewhere in the Carpathians. (*Photo R. Vishniak*)

). Jewish lumbermen, Bustina. (*Photo R. Vishniak*)

11. Title page of *Beis Yisroel* with portrait of R. Mendele Hager, first Vishnitzer Rebbe, Sziget, 1939.

12. Title page of *Lider fun Mein Lebn* by Hirsch Leib Gottlieb with portrait of the author, Seaini, 1933.

Sziget, 12. Jan. 1894. „JÜDISCHE VOLKSZEITUNG.“ II. Jahrgang Nro 1

Vierteljährig 1 fl. יידישע בצײַטי Erscheint jeden Freitag

פאלקסצײַטונג

Organ für Handel und jüdische Interessen.

Erscheint einmal wöchentlich, jeden Freitag.
Abonnements-Preis: ganzjährig 4 fl. halbjährig 2 fl. vierteljährig 1 fl. Einzelne Nummern 8 kr.
Adresse: „Jüdische Volkezeitung“ M.-Sziget.

צווייטער יאָרגאַנג נומער 1. הירש ליב נאסעליעב

Masthead of *Yiddishe Volkszeitung*, Sziget, 1894.

II. Evfo'yın 40 szám. „ZION“ M.-Sziget, 1903. Julius 6.

Megjelen.
hetenként egyszer,
minden
csütörtökön.
Előfizetési ár:
félévre — — 4 kor
negyedévre — 2 »
egyes szám — 20 fil.

ציון

Társadalmi és szépirodalmi hetilap.

צווייטער יאָרגאַנג נ"ר. 40. הירש ליב נאַסעליעב.

Masthead of *Zion*, Sziget, 1903.

Felelős kiadó:
Reich Jehosua;
Szerk. és kiadóhivatal:
Tel-Aviv, Stand u. 14;

Telefon 221740;
Bankszámla:
Bank-Hámizráchi, 7250
T.-A., Lilienblum u. 48
Posta Bankszámla 44190.

מרמרוש-סיגעט
MARAMAROSSZIGET

לא למכירה

1967. DECEMBER בסלו תשכ"ח KIADJA: „IRGUN MÁRMAROSSZIGET B’ISRAEL“. VIII. ÉVF. — 34 szám

Masthead of *Mármarossziget*, Tel-Aviv, 1967.

16. Page from the First Graduation Yearbook of the Hebrew Gymnasium of Mukacevo, 1932.

7. The final destination: Auschwitz.

8. German civilians forced by U.S. soldiers to view corpses of Nazi victims.

19. Father and son at work in a New York factory.

20. Holocaust survivor in the service of the community, Williamsburg, U.S.A.

A typical scene on Lee Avenue in the heart of Williamsburg.

Throngs at the funeral of Rabbi Yoel Teitelbaum, 1979, Monroe, N.Y. (*N.Y. Daily News photo*)

23. Memorial plaques on Mt. Zion, Jerusalem for the destroyed
Jewish communities of the Carpathians (clockwise):
Ungvár, Munkács, Spinka, Mármaros-Sziget

PART II

THE PEOPLE

HERZL (HERMAN) APSAN

Long before meeting the children of Herzl Apsan in New York, I had already decided to translate two chapters of his book for inclusion in "Piety and Perseverance." Then, when I spoke to Alter and Dora, his children, and Howie, his grandson, I was very touched by their gracious endorsement of my plans. In fact, Dora, a physician in Valhalla, New York, shared with me the yet unpublished family history from which many details have been culled.

Her father was born in 1886 in Remeti, a village near Sziget, where he received his early education. He then moved on to the well-known Yeshivah of Pápa, Hungary, where he also managed to obtain a good secular grounding in the Hungarian and German languages, plus the study of bookkeeping. Upon return to Sziget, he, together with a young friend, opened up an office; it seems, however, that the local lawyers contended the office was unauthorized and forced it to close. In 1908, Apsan moved to the small community of Koenigsfeld where he married and became a wheat merchant, travelling all throughout Hungary, including its capital, Budapest. Apparently village life did not appeal to him; by 1914 he had moved back to Sziget. During World War I, he served, was decorated and promoted to Sergeant in the Hungarian Army. Misfortune, however, had struck his home. His wife, mother of his three children, had died, and in 1919 Apsan married for the second time. His choice was Zisl

153

Basch, a twenty-one-year-old from nearby Spinka, the community known by the Hasidic dynasty of the same name to which the young bride was related through her father. From this marriage Apsan had five more children. Let us hear what his oldest and only daughter has to write about the family:

Father was always overwhelmed by the burden of providing for a growing family. Mike [second son of the first wife] who was studying in Temesvár used to say that whenever he would come home on vacation there would be a new baby in his mother's arms. Over the years, Father tried several businesses; first, fruit exporting, then grain exporting. We lived in a two-room apartment and the kitchen was always filled with grain and flour. Later on, he rented a store on the Yiddish street and for many years was a grain merchant. During the last few years, he tried the life insurance business and had a small office. I still don't know who needed life insurance in Sighet, nevertheless, he convinced many well-to-do people to sign up and pay the small monthly installments. It was my job after school on Fridays, to go from store to store collecting these payments. They always made excuses for delaying their payments, which caused me great aggravation.

Father was known as a straightforward and honest man, and he was often called upon to arbitrate conflicts where his fair and objective opinion was always appreciated. They also knew him for the stories he would tell at the coffeehouses where people sat around and listened to him for hours. At home on Saturdays, he would tell the same stories about the life of the Jews in Máramaros. He became known as the "story-teller of Máramaros," or "the Sholom Aleichem of Máramaros."

About the book itself, a loving daughter has this to say:

Father had finally published his first book in Yiddish, entitled, The Story of the Rabbi from Vishnitz, which was actually a collection of stories about the Jews in Máramaros and how they would go on pilgrimages to this Rabbi during the High Holy Days. The book did not sell too well, and Father had to travel to Transylvania and Hungary to promote it. When he made some money, he would come home to the family and stay as long as the money lasted. He was also writing stories for subsequent books which were never published. He read a great deal of Yiddish literature, newspapers and also studied our history and science texts which he found very stimulating.

The two chapters selected for translation show Apsan as the fine and warm writer that he was. His intimate description of Hasidic life reflects himself, a participant as well as an observer of the scene.

THE SPECIAL HIGH HOLY DAY TRAIN

"I still had my whole dowry in my pocket," thus he continued his story, "and from the entire neighborhood I got together with and selected a popular group of young people, go-getters, singers, merrymakers, worshippers and Bible readers. They were all well-fed young men in their first year of marriage and still eating Kest in their in-laws' homes. We hired a strong horse and carriage and traveled overnight into the city of Sziget."

And so began another chapter. Everywhere on the platform, in the railroad station and in all waiting rooms, first, second and third-class, and, in addition, in the street stood long-frocked Hasidic Jews with small packages and bundles waiting for the special train to depart. The Hasidim had rented a locomotive with wagon upon wagon from the Railroad Department in Debrecen. It was to be a Jewish public domain for five whole days from the day before Rosh Hashanah until the Fast of Gedaliah, a permanent home for Hasidim on their journey to Vishnitz and back.

Nachman Hofman of the Visheve was now the Director of the train; Shlomo Yosef Miller, the train leader and administrator; Herzl, the son-in-law of Chana, the treasurer; Lazar Yorovits together with Ezra Moshe Miller were in charge of drinks. They brought along small barrels of beer with large bottles of refreshments, "Shelish," with plum brandy to sell to the people at a fair price throughout the whole journey. In addition, there were reliable men, inspectors with brakemen, railroadmen and conductors and comptrollers, all Vishnitzer Hasidim. A genuine Jewish government, Jewish leadership with a Jewish train, Jewish billets, train tickets with Jewish leaders and their signatures, just as in our Holy City of Jerusalem in the days of the Temple.

As soon as everybody was aboard and settled in the wagons, the chimney of the locomotive let out a big loud

156

whistle, sounding off brazenly and proudly: "All of you remain healthy and hope that you will have a good year!" A nod to all and soon departed. "And the children of Israel left [Egypt] with a high hand (Exodus 14:8)." Jews departed in a very good mood, with a full and joyous heart. Little by little the train disappeared, farther and farther, smaller and smaller, until it completely faded between the high mountains . . . then it was gone. Only clouds of smoke hovered over the fields and on the mountains, a reminder that the special train had just left the city.

As soon as the train reached the end of the city, past the salt mill and the Szigeter Chamber, Jews began wiping their hands on the windowpanes. Many had water flasks in their packs; soon someone stood before a prayer stand near the window facing East. A Minyan was speedily formed and the Jews recited the Psalms. Some studied Mishnah and others said special prayers for a safe journey; some engaged in performing a Mitzvah by going from compartment to compartment, wagon to wagon, and collecting contributions. One carried his money in a bandana, one threw donations for a sick person, a family man with many children who had become greatly impoverished and forced to remain at home.

Jews continuously went from door to door, wagon to wagon, freely, singly or two together; no one was afraid of anybody; it was all in one domain under the government of the Hasidim from Vishnitz and Máramaros. They busied themselves with matters pertaining to their Jewish faith, not idling away their time, but always with a holy book in the hand.

At every station, Bitshkev, Rachov, Jasina up until the Polish border, other well-known good brethren, Vishnitzer Hasidim, came aboard with their valises and knapsacks filled with clothes for the Holidays and food for the journey. They were escorted to the train by their wives and children, who gave them various petitions to remember when seeking advice from the Rebbe. There was joy and a friendly "Hello" in every corner of the train. People became acquainted and enjoyed each other's company, making room for each other in the tight and narrow space, and traveling with a great white pennant inscribed, "Banner of the Camp of Israel!" It fluttered above the train with dignity and pride, informing the whole world: "Here we are, Jews of Máramaros traveling to Vishnitz with scarcely a single Hasid remaining at home."

They journeyed over the Carpathian mountains and through dark tunnels. They traveled over long iron bridges and great mountains, high over the top. Once they viewed the villages from above and another time it was just the opposite. At every stop Jews came to greet the travelers and give them petitions and donations for the Rebbe. They spoke in confidence, entrusting them with different private matters. They wished each other a Blessed New Year, joining together with the Rebbe towards the speedy advent of the Messiah.

In Delatyn, a small city in Galicia, the special train had to wait on the open platform for quite some time, for the traffic there was heavy. Trains and locomotives came and went, with whistles and snorts, puffing heavily and panting sadly. The whole engine sweating and the steam dripping from every part. The traffic was heavy and the work was great. We were unable to leave until a newly-fired engine was attached to our train, and that entailed waiting until several other trains left for different countries in the big, wide world. Jews ran from the train to fill their bottles with drinking water, attending to their physical needs and then washing their hands before meals.

Jews purchased a little anisette whiskey, Polish merchandise, and mingled amid the large crowd, among the Poles and Ukrainians. They all stared at the white banner inscribed, "Banner of the Camp of Israel!" which decorated and beautified the whole train, and looked surprised to see so many thousands of Jews with long beards and sidecurls.

In the meantime, a group of Jews—the "let's go" type— got together on the platform and began dancing in the joyful, good-natured Vishnitzer style. They placed one hand on the other man's shoulder and another under the ear. They danced and sang with their eyes closed:

> And purify our hearts to serve Thee in truth
> To serve Thee, to serve Thee in truth
>
> And purify our hearts, to serve Thee in truth,
> To serve Thee in truth, to serve Thee
> To serve Thee in truth.

All Poles, civilian officials and military officers with their ladies, as well as noble travelers and ordinary folk looked on and felt as useless as the dust of the earth; now no one had the dominance nor the power nor the word; they did not dare to say anything bad about Jewish people, they all just stared as Jews danced for the sake of the Heaven above.

The conductors whistling and signalling their flags announce the train's departure, but the Jews do not stop. They continue dancing in front of all the people, no one dreams of travelling on — then the stationmaster himself approaches them with all his dignity and courtesy; "Gentlemen, the train must leave. All aboard!" And he begs them compassionately and pleadingly to stop the dancing, but the Jews still pay no attention; "What right does he have and how dare he order a Jewish train about?" And all make fun of him and laugh in his face.

One husky merrymaker runs towards him and pushes the bottle of Shelish under his nose and shouts, "L'Chaim, to Life, Boss. Let us all have a good Year and let the Messiah come soon." He taps him on the shoulder and all laugh, enjoying themselves heartily at his nerve.

And the official becomes shrunken and scared before the many Hasidim who are all dancing happily. He begins to think that the days of the Messiah are truly here, and against his will also joins in the laughter. Then, as soon as all are finally aboard, the locomotive lets loose a very shrill whistle sounding off in train language, "Jews and Gentiles, begging the distinction, all of you keep healthy, we have to go on," and surely the train finally moves from the spot.

It is already deep night, the sky is cloudy for it is the end of the month and God's world is completely darkened in a dense cloud. Whole camps, just like the pillar of cloud in the days of our Teacher Moses, travel through distant places and strange lands, all covered by the stars in the sky; nobody knows whence they come and where they go so late in the night. The veil of the night wraps the whole world in a dream, and God, the Creator and Leader of the whole world, looks on with love just like a mother who puts her beloved children to sleep. Now all His creatures are resting. Somewhere one hears a lonely bird crying deep in the woods, complaining before the Keeper of the Forest, but no one understands his complaint. The frogs in the marshes have already finished their nightly prayers, and have stopped their croak, croak. All have moved to the side on a shore, close their eyes and go to sleep. Now the whole universe is asleep.

It is strangely quiet all around the whole horizon, on fields and roads, on mountains and valleys. One no longer hears the movement of a bird or the sound of a car. It is already midnight, simple and honest working Jews sleep throughout the journey in small wooden cubicles. Everybody sleeps and snores in his corner; everyone is worn and tired out from the never-ending labors.

Soon half the night is gone and the sky is beginning to light up on the horizon. The moon carries out God's command to shine over the entire world. He is the permanent Guardian of Israel, he never goes astray, never oversleeps or even closes an eye; he crawls out of the clouds soon after midnight, just like a thief, without any noise or movement. He wipes his eyes and mirrors his face in the great waters, and takes over his nightly duties. He rises from the south and moves northward, circling the whole world. He makes great strides, thousands of miles per minute; he pours out thousands, millions of tons of light, over valleys and mountains, across oceans and deserts. He looks into all fields and forests, overhears all secrets and is familiar with all the hidden happenings of the dark night.

From nowhere a group of bees arrives strayed from foreign lands, running and humming, buzzing and searching for a place to rest, but not daring to set down in an unknown place. And a group of soft winds waft from the East and travels through the forests up to the river Sambatyon and the lands of Eternity. All wander into warm lands, listening to every sound and every movement in the forest, telling lovely tales in their native tongue and language: news from one country and another; which rites and customs are observed by these Jews in their homes, which souls and migrants move about without redemption over all paths, lanes, walks and steps; whom they met and what they encountered in the quiet Selichot night.

And a heavily laden Special Train with Hasidim from the whole of Máramaros chases and runs, puffs and works with all parts; the wheels turn and the axles moan and squeak from dryness and heat. The locomotive sweats, makes noise and whistles, letting loose from the chimney a dense black smoke with sparks of fire, with drops of sweat pouring out from every particle. Chambers of metal and walls of tin roofs race vehemently, cutting across strong mountains through tunnels of iron, splitting and crossing all lakes and waters, straightening out the whole world. Everything and everyone does his work with perfection, enthusiasm and dedication in honor of the many Hasidim and their Rebbe and in honor of the great God of Israel.

It is already late. Half the night is gone; it does not stand still but inches forward. Old Hasidim who cannot sleep, already count every second out of sheer boredom. Everyone is fearful of being late for the *Zechor B'rith* prayer with the Rebbe at his Court. Somewhere in the distance one can hear a

sleepy rooster with a hoarse "kikeri'ki"; he doesn't open his
eyes and is too lazy to rise so early — but when Jews hear the
sound of the rooster, the whole village arises for the *Selichot*
prayers.

And here in the train, there is a yawning and stretching
on all sides. One stretches all his limbs and shakes off the
sleep, while some are still snoring and resting with their
elbows on other peoples' shoulders. All seats are crowded.
The train twists and turns. The young men are still asleep and
snoring throughout the whole train.

The Hasidim begin to nudge each other, "Up! Get up
Jews, we are almost in Vishnitz." And soon a moving and a
commotion commences, an awakening with washing of
hands, a pushing and a tumult in all parts of the wagons. One
jumps from the seats to the shelves, from one seat over a
second and across a third; everyone grabs his little valise, his
bag with his knapsack; one ties, binds and passes it along.
There are calls from all sides: "Shmuel, Shabtai, Chaim! Do
you have everything? Make sure not to leave any belongings
in the train!" They all herd together and push and shove
towards the doors. Everyone wants to be the first to rush out
of the train. They open the windows and the doors, tripping
over piled-up packages, valises and knapsacks. They look
through the windows, attempting to get a glimpse of the
city and soon there is motion and excitement all over the
train.

Brothers-in-law, brothers with parents and relatives, in-
laws with ordinary neighbors and good friends from their
home towns do not want to get lost and hold on to each other,
shouting with all tones of voices: "Where are you, where are
you? And you, where are you? Do you have the Bible? The
Mishnayis and the *Gartl* [Belt]?" And all want to hold on to
each other and together ride into the city.

Then, a weak, hoarse sound with a sleepy whistle soon
informs the city folks that the train has arrived. The pillar of
cloud has moved into the rear, into another land, and the

pillar of fire from the gas lamps of the city suddenly begins to throw light on the wagons and into the eyes of the Jews, and suddenly the station is in front of us. "Vishnitz!" call the conductors on the platform, "Vishnitz!"

The whole city is now awakened by the Lord, the Almighty Himself! Not through an angel, and not through a messenger; No, He Himself in His majestic glory jumps over Jewish homes and streets, inspecting the whole household of Israel. This night is for Jews, the Great Night of Prayer and Repentance in the entire wide world wherever there are Jews, and in particular here in Vishnitz. The Almighty Himself takes care so that God forbid no harm should come upon Jews today, and He sees how Jewish children, Jews from different provinces and far away countries have come together to repent, confess and to give a complete accounting on this great and awesome day of New Year at the Rebbe's Court.

In all homes and rooms of the city there is now commotion, no one has even closed his eyes. It is light in the houses, light in the Bet Hamidrash, light in all the windows and light all over the streets so that one could even inspect pearls in every street of the city.

They come and go, go and come; they arrange the rooms, they move things this way and that way, and soon back again; they prepare for the Hasidim. Men and women with children, all are in disarray. They carry tables and benches, plates and spoons from neighbors and stores. One lends and borrows all the best in the entire city. Young and old prepare and perspire in every house. They cook, bake, fry and sweat, men, women and servants in the kitchen of every house. In the meantime, they take a quick glance through the windows and doors to view the traffic out in the street.

Everyone counts or estimates the large number of people that has been brought by train from Poland, the Bukovina and all places; with Isaac from Rumania, Novoselica from Russia and the Special Train from Máramaros, which has just arrived.

Fiacres and carriages, old and new, ornate and decrepit, with plain horses and carts, one-horse carriages, besides porters and guides with agents for boarding houses and modern hotels with restaurants, all are covering the whole neighborhood, the whole platform of the railroad station.

Everyone was eager and ready to earn a living, one watched the many Hasidim who had been brought here by train from all parts; the entire Hasidic world had been set into motion; they had all come to pray with the Rebbe on the day before the New Year, and no able-bodied soul stayed home.

Suddenly, there was a heavy outpouring of the Hasidim from the wagons and the station, not just one or two at once, but a world full of Hasidim, small, tall, young, old, Hasidim with caps and hats, with collars, coats and caftans, all mixed together and coming from all sides. The entire neighborhood was covered at once. The whole street was suddenly darkened from the shadows and blackened by people, filled up with Jews with packs, knapsacks, cases, bundles and valises. They ran, chased, pushed and rushed. They jumped head on through the gates and the waiting room, without any plan or order. Everyone runs and flies, pushing faster and faster, one ahead of the second and the third, straight into the city. They run and move more with their hands than with their feet. They scarcely catch their breath running, they want to quickly grab a good place to stay, a good inn, where one can rest his head for the whole Holiday. They also quickly make a dash for the ritual bath and afterwards bid welcome to the Rebbe, and listen to his Selichot prayers.

No one asks the price of a carriage or a seat, one does not argue, one jumps on the fiacre, whoever can grabs a place first, two, three or four on one seat. One above and one below, one in the front and one in the rear and one on the driver's seat, even standing on the steps, just to keep going. One calls out to a comrade, a neighbor, a relative, a good companion, "Quick, quick, just jump on! Shemuel, Yankel with Moshe, here we live as good neighbors." One has thrown a covered basket containing all his belongings, including his fur hat, onto the top seat, and then they all disappear into the city.

Clouds of dust begin to rise in the sky from the big tumult and running, and there was choking and commotion all through the street. Jews drive into the clouds; everything burst and crashed under their feet, and they still kept on running.

From the train up to the city there was now busy hustling, talking and shouting, just as the Great Fair in the month of Elul before the High Holidays. This night was the night of holy watching. One did not see a stranger on the entire street, only Hasidim who came to repent and to pray together with the Rebbe throughout the Holiday. A hurrying and racing by, Jews with fiacres and small carriages; not for a single minute does the street remain idle or empty.

Cars run in and soon return; every fiacre and carriage wants to utilize the time and opportunity and at least turn around five to six or even seven times, to carry the people from the train into the city. Not every day or even every week is the traffic so heavy. They have been awaiting this for many weeks. They have gone into debt on this account in every store for corn, meat and bread. Everyone pushes and rushes, they almost race themselves to death, chasing and speeding, loaded down front and rear, up and down through the street. The horses jump and run with their heads proudly held high, brazenly; they know and seem to understand the greatness of this night. They will eat and rest another time when there will be more leisure or nothing else to do altogether. Jews jump into the air; then four, five and even six fiacres move through the width of the street at once. They do not call anyone; they just fall upon the fiacres from all sides, just as bees upon honey; they accept any price asked, there is no time for arguing, making deals or setting conditions. The Hasidim are being skinned alive.

THE AFTERNOON BEFORE ROSH HASHANAH

The whole afternoon the learned Hasidim moved around in the *Bet Hamidrash*, and in the Rebbe's Court. They looked around to see who else had arrived: new Hasidim who had never before been to Vishnitz; young men, recently married, who still ate in their in-laws' houses and came at their expense. They extended greetings and soon became acquainted, inquiring about the father-in-law, his background and that of the son, where the other Jews of their village had gone, the Shochet, the Dayan or even the Rabbi himself, and whether this year there were more learned sons-in-law. In short, one sought news about the whole village.

Matchmakers perspired running from one inn to another, laboring hard in bringing together future in-laws, first inquiring after the names of the men, then the women, the name of the bride (they must not have the same name — legacy of Rabbi Yehuda, the Pious). They examined prospective bridegrooms and their knowledge of the *Shulchan Aruch*, and of a difficult portion in the Talmudic commentaries. They sought the advice of the Rebbe and the counsel of the children; they agreed on the dowry and set a date, where and when the groom and the bride should meet to see and be seen, mostly at the big annual fairs of Tatsheve or Sziget. When the conversation warmed up, the in-laws liked each other and the Rebbe gave his consent, then the whole matter was settled by a handshake. They all went home with the match almost complete. In-laws, about to finish the marriage preparations, discussed when both parties should visit the city to purchase the bridal gifts. Poorer in-laws talked about how many guests to invite and how much food to prepare. "I, for one," said one of them, "will not burden you, I will only bring two carloads of guests, one for the men, the groom and some of his young friends. The Shochet and a few neighbors in one car, and in the other, the women. Enough! We don't need any more."

A more well-to-do in-law, who wanted to make a big show and bring his important relatives, said, "Mechutan (in-law), this has been the custom in our family! When one prepares for the wedding of a child and the Almighty has helped him thus far, he invites all his good friends from the village. I expect to come with eight to ten small carriages of relatives, our family — may it be protected from the evil eye — is large and I do not intend to insult anyone. Just prepare a lot to drink and you will see what merrymakers our Jews are and how they can entertain bridegroom and bride."

Simple, far from scholarly people, storekeepers and traders in general, roamed through the city the whole afternoon, each to his class, his profession and his trade. A clothing trader soon turned up at a local textile dealer, looked at his bales of merchandise asking the price of flax, linen and cloth, whether peddlers bring new flax and where they trade it all. "In our area," he said, "the prices for new flax and linen are very low, and, in general, there is strong competition in every piece of cloth and no chance for profit. When the non-Jew has an old piece of cloth or footwear, soon after Passover when the weather warms up, he brings them to the Jewish storekeeper and trades them for kerosene, oil, maize and flour. One trader pays more than the other and soon every Jew becomes a dealer of cloth."

A good look at the bale of cloth and soon the following question is asked: "Are there any Ruthenians living in this area?" He had recognized the many pieces of house linen with special embroideries, all that a peasant likes to wear. As soon as they saw that they were talking to an experienced businessman, a lively conversation developed, and one told the other, "Here we have a great deal of competition and one always has to invent new tricks that the other party does not know." And he talks about the linen that he selects for home use, clean white pieces and machine products. They then discuss the whole process in all its phases. This is being sent to the big factories and mills, and that to the threshing machines. There is great demand for this merchandise today, and it fetches a good price. The gray flax is good for making blankets in the factory and he mentions the address. The other assortment goes to Lemberg and from there by train to Vienna.

Cotton merchants entered a store, looked at a bale of merchandise and asked the following question: "Why is this so poorly bleached? This wouldn't sell by us; the peasant likes sound merchandise. When he has good cloth, he can make good towels and tablecloths for Jews and their daughters, and get a good price, but your quality he would be unable to sell." As soon as the other sees that he talks to an expert he tells him, "The competition between traders here is very strong. Every Jew opens a store and sells everything cheaper and cheaper. He is already down to his bare capital. He has to work with such merchandise to be competitive and to earn five Groschen at each package." After they get to know each other better, they find the address of the manufacturer and they write it down on a slip of paper. His name is Hans Mahler from Hausdorf, a small city in Bohemia, near Eger.

A horsetrader hurried about among the fiacres and carriages, discovering a pair of black horses hitched onto a carriage. "Where did you get these two singers?" asked the trader with a smile. One could see that the Hasid was a trader who understood horses for he grabbed a horse by its head, turned it towards himself and inspected its teeth. Soon he was told that these horses had been bought from a Count. They had been military horses, marching and standing with military discipline and pride. They ran like the wind and pulled the heaviest loads, but they had one fault: as soon as they heard martial music, no matter how important their trip, they would stop and start to dance according to the melody and rhythm. No whipping or beating would help the situation.

Soon the Hasid told this story of a white horse and what troubles he had with it. In the middle of a journey it got annoyed and stubbornly refused to move. No one knew why it stopped and stood on its hind legs, refusing to budge. They beat it, but it pushed and pushed, turning the carriage around and throwing off the reins from its hind legs until the frightened passengers clambered out of the carriage.

Another time he had it shoed at the local blacksmith, but the nail pierced its foot. From then on the white horse limped, and they were forced to sell it in the market to gypsies, barely receiving the value of its skin. To this very day, no one knows whether the gypsies succeeded in treating the horse with home remedies or not, the Hasid concluded, and everyone regarded him as one who knew how to tell a good horse story!

Soon all coach drivers descended from their fiacres and gathered around the Hasid. They talked and talked for a long time about all kinds of horses and their encounters with them. Thus, they all became very well acquainted with each other.

Somewhere in a corner one said quietly to another, pointing his finger, "You see Brother Shabbatai, this is a better world with more decent people where this Jew lives. Here, a carriage driver, a coach driver or a horse trader can show his face among people, among Hasidim or the general community. Not so with us, where as soon as something happens people shout accusingly, 'You coach driver, you low class, you horse thief!' " And this Hasid with his stories made all of them feel very good.

Produce merchants walked into a flour shop and examined the flour. They asked, "What grade is this or that? Is it good for baking and does it require a lot of water when used for baking? Does it contain enough gluten?" "With us," one said, "everything comes from the area near the river Tisa that has all the advantages. Its wheat is of the 82 to 85 points quality and famous in the whole world."

Soon the storekeeper showed fine flour from the good earth of Stanislau and Lemberg; due to the keen competition he also had to keep a cheaper quality on hand. Bread baked from flour mixed with oats and barley is very much liked by the peasants for it needs little yeast.

The Hasid swiftly took a few kernels of maize and bit them with his front teeth, but promptly spat them out owing to their bitter taste. "Where did you get such poor maize?" he asked after putting a few kernels to his nose and sniffing them. "They are moldy and smell like glue," he exclaimed. "They are without color and not fully ripe. Where I come from we have a wide assortment of maize. Your variety could never be sold by us. Our peasant wants the flour for his bread to be fiery red; he would not even feed such bitter and gluey merchandise to his horse!"

"No," comes the retort, "we here live near Novoselica, the maize comes from across the border of Russia. It is all cheap, but our peasant is already accustomed to it. He never ate any better maize, and also uses it to feed his horses that do not mind either. Perhaps it is even better for it can be chewed easily and tastes more like grass and soil."

And as the talking continues, they soon learn more news about the maize that is being brought from Russia with rubels and kopeks. The agents at the Exchange in Novoselica bring the traders across the border; they settle on the price and personally inspect their purchases. They then store the maize in caves, which gives it an earthy taste. So much maize is grown that there is a shortage of sacks and barns. And at the Exchange in Novoselica, money changes hands daily, sometimes cheaper and sometimes dearer. There is never a fixed price. And there is a world of banks: the Wiener Bank Verein, the Handelsbank or the Credit Bank of Vienna. They accredit the merchandise and only send it after a substantial down payment has been made.

And thus matters became clearer and addresses were exchanged. A few purchased some merchandise that was convenient; they found some good and inexpensive shoes, pieces of cloth and fashions, which they carried home with them.

HIRSCH LEIB GOTTLIEB

Hirsch Leib Gottlieb was a professional jester who performed his own skits at Purim celebrations. The following seven paragraphs represent a humorous pun about card playing on Chanukah. It is phrased in the ambiguous language of the legal profession.

THE SEVEN LAWS GOVERNING CARD PLAYING

Paragraph 1. Everyone is permitted to gamble on Chanukah, even Rabbis, Ritual Slaughterers and Cantors. Should one begin playing on Friday and it gets late, one may continue for three hours into the Sabbath. This is the custom, and a custom is stronger than the Law of observing the Sabbath.
Commentary: Often such a custom is strong enough to destroy the gambler's spirit, for when he loses his money, he looks like a mourner (with a bowed head.)

Paragraph 2. Q. When does one begin playing cards in honor of Chanukah?

A. Soon after the festival of Sukkoth, i.e. two months before Chanukah, and until Passover, i.e. approx. four months after Chanukah. Some observant ones begin playing with the sound of the Shofar in the month of Elul, i.e. 45 days before Sukkoth, but the *very* observant ones commence during the Nine Days before the Fast of Tisha B'Av, i.e. 30 days

before the Blowing of the Shofar. They also use the Mourning
Melody (Echa) when conversing.

Paragraph 3. It is better to play in someone else's home
so that the wife and children become fed up with waiting.
The playing should commence a few minutes before dusk
and continue until the morning star rises. (The very observant play until after the hour for the Shema Prayer, in compliance with the Law that he who fulfills one commandment
is freed from fulfilling another.) And finally, he for whom
playing is his major occupation, is allowed to play all day
long, provided of course that there is someone to play with.

Paragraph 4. It is better to play in a restaurant where food
and drink are available, but in an emergency, private homes
may be substituted. And although one leaves such homes like
a burned person, this does not matter, for one's food budget is
fixed in Heaven on New Year, but money for card playing is
unlimited. Here is proof positive: We find people who are
stingy with pennies, but don't mind losing large sums when
playing, as it is written in Scriptures: One always finds
enough for the Devil.

Paragraph 5. When playing cards the prohibition against
stealing and robbing does not become operative according to
the Talmudic law which states that only one prohibition at a
time may be operative. Therefore, one may steal at cards or
change cards or lie about money, even move over someone
else's money. When playing cards, there is no commandment
of "Honor Thy Father"; to steal from one's Father enhances
the beauty of the commandment. Many have the custom to
tell their father when playing, "Father, you should lie down
like a dog ..." and some children address their Father in
these words, "This card will bury you"; or, "This card will
put you in the ground." A famous player told me why the
commandment of "Honor Thy Father" does not apply to
cards ... the commandment of "Honor Thy Father" speaks
about long life, which is not present when playing cards.
Here time runs out fast.

Paragraph 6. When one loses all his money, he may deposit a pawn, but only when the pawnshop is closed; otherwise, even though the shop may be a distance, he must go to the shop to get cash.

Paragraph 7. Since the Angels do not understand Yiddish, it is customary to name cards in the Holy Hebrew language. "Queens" are called *"Nekevot"* (Females); "Aces" are called *"Zetim"* (Olives) or *"Betzim"* (Eggs); "Kings" are called plain *"Melachim"* (Kings). The very observant say *"Vaya'avor"* (And He passed) for "Pass." The story is told of Rabbi Gambler, the Great, who had played all through the night prior to the Fast of the Tenth of Teveth. In the morning he fell asleep during the Penitential prayers in the Synagogue. Thus, so tell the Hasidim, his soul went up to Heaven; suddenly he heard the Cantor chant aloud, "Vaya'avor." The Rabbi jumped up shouting: "Why Vaya'avor? I have three Zetim!"

A CRAZY LAW SUIT
(The Cow or the Sister)

No sooner had Motele, the Rabbi of B_____, returned from the synagogue with his *Talith* bag under his arm, than he found Bentsin Czobyrk waiting for him. Bentsin had come to the rabbi on a religious law suit either to question or merely to seek advice. But I can assure you, dear Reader, that poor Bentsin — it should not happen in this day — had been hit with a doubly great misfortune, to wit:

Shmeryl, who lives a *Techum Sabbath* away from Bentsin, [a distance of 2000 ells, which religious Jews are not permitted to exceed when walking out of town on the Sabbath] stole and ran off with Bentsin's cow on Saturday night. If he had only escaped with the cow, Bentsin's bad luck would not have been so great. The misfortune was that Shmeryl also took Benstin's sister, a young widow. On this account the distressed Bentsin came to the Rabbi of B _____ to pour out his heavy heart.

Rabbi Motele asked Bentsin to sit down and recount all that had happened to him. Now, dear Reader, let both speak, the Rabbi and Bentsin, and let us see whether they understand each other.

Bentsin:	Rabbi! My sister and my cow, they were both with me, she was a widow . . .
Rabbi:	Who, the cow? . . .
Benstin:	No, the sister was a widow. Suddenly Shmeryl comes and takes her with him which caused me great loss for she gave me so much milk every day . . .
Rabbi:	Who, the sister?
Bentsin:	No, the cow!
Rabbi:	I don't understand you, Bentsin. You said "sister" before . . .

Bentsin:	You should be well, Rabbi. He also took the sister after he untied the rope from her horns . . .
Rabbi:	Whose? . . . the sister's?
Bentsin:	I told you already, the cow's, she has already given me so much milk — the cow, not the sister — and she used to say the prayers with the children, I mean the sister, not the cow. And she was a precious diamond . . .
Rabbi:	The cow?
Bentsin:	No, the sister. And now I don't know what to do. She was worth about 30 silver crowns, a fat animal . . .
Rabbi:	You undoubtedly mean the cow? . . .
Bentsin:	Whom else, the sister? Now, dear Rabbi, what shall I do? Unfortunately, she was a widow; she had no other fault except she used to kick with her legs . . .
Rabbi:	Who? . . . the sister?
Bentsin:	For Heaven's sake, what is the matter with you, Rabbi? Why do you mix up the cow with the sister?
Rabbi:	Now, what do you want? A judgment on the sister or on the cow? . . .
Bentsin:	For both . . .
Rabbi:	So go ahead and bring me the cow and the sister . . .
Bentsin:	If I had been able to bring them, I would not have come here . . .
Rabbi:	If so, you are right, go and bring Shmeryl . . .
Bentsin:	Shmeryl also disappeared like a puff of smoke. Don't forget all that remains is a calf which she left behind . . .
Rabbi:	Who? The sister? . . .
Bentsin:	(grabs his cane and runs out shouting . . .) For God's sake, the cow, not the sister!

The Rabbi remained alone, deep in thought and humming a Talmudic melody, murmuring to himself as follows:

Let us see, I have here before me, a cow, a widow that says prayers with the children, and a milk-giving sister that kicks. How does this come to pass? There is Shmeryl who stole the sister and he left a calf and escaped with the widow . . . If I say that the sister is the widow, how does a calf come to her? Therefore, I must say that the cow is the widow, but why then does the sister kick? Upon my life, this is a difficult decision, from cow, sister . . . sister and cow . . .!

RABBI ISRAEL HAGER

Rabbi Israel Hager (1860-1936), was known as
THE SABBA KADISHA (Holy Old Man). These stories
are translated from the Hebrew Kedosh Yisrael,
ed. E. Roth, Bne Brak, 1976, V. I & II.

Month of Elul

During the month of Elul the Rebbe would daily recite the entire Book of Psalms at the conclusion of the morning service, except on Friday and Sabbath.

One time, a father and his son, both Shochetim, came to spend the Sabbath under the roof of the Sabba Kadisha. On Sunday, they prayed in his company and then prepared to return home. The Sabba Kadisha strolled back and forth in the Bet Hamidrash, reciting the Psalms with great devotion. The two Shochetim listened to his words that flowed into them as fresh water quenches a tired and thirsty soul. The son complained to his father that they would be denied the privilege of the Rabbi's company for the High Holidays. (The Shochetim lived far distant and had to be back on their jobs.) Thus, they would be unable to enjoy the sweet prayers and melodies of the Rebbe.

But when the Sabba Kadisha came to the Special High Holiday Psalm, "*L'David Mizmor*," he paused by the son and sang it in the High Holiday melody. At the conclusion of the

Psalm, the Rebbe said, "Now that you have heard L'David Mizmor, you may return home in peace and contentment."

Love of Jews

Thus were the ways of the Rebbe — to love every Jew in Israel as he was. When the Rebbe was asked by one of the great Rabbis of his time whether he takes contributions from a Jew who does not observe the Sabbath, he expressed surprise, "And how does His Honor feel about this?" Answered the Rabbi, "I do not take. I first ask whether this Jew observed the Sabbath or not."

Commented the Rebbe afterwards, "My way is as follows: I prefer not to ask and risk learning that the Jew does not observe the Sabbath, thus hearing something bad about a Jew. I prefer to take the money and give it to the Government for tax purposes."

Sabba Kadisha's love for people was particularly evident in Grosswardein (Rumania), where there were many Ashkenazic Jews who opposed the Hasidic influence. They were afraid that it would cause strife within the community due to the change in religious customs. But our Holy Rebbe, through his wisdom, love of people and love of peace, turned his enemies into friends.

He was known to have said, 'I love them so much until they start to love me."

Rabbi Chaim Elazar Spira [the fiery Rebbe of Munkács] once told the Rebbe that he suffers a great deal from the Hasidim of his city. To which the Rebbe replied, "Do as I did in Grosswardein; I loved my opponents so much that they started to love me."

Visiting the Sick

The Holy Old Man used to make every effort to visit the sick in his community. In certain cases he used to travel far in order to comfort an ailing soul.

One day, a pious person who had never set foot in the house of the Holy Man fell ill. The Holy Old Man proceeded at once to visit the patient. When those close to the Rebbe urged him not to go, he pushed them aside, saying, "When I feel that a Jew doesn't love me, I treat him kindly until he does so."

Providing for the Dowry

Once a poor man approached the Rebbe complaining that although he had received a fine marriage offer for his daughter, he did not know how he would manage to obtain a dowry for her.

The Rebbe invited him to come the following day when a timber merchant would seek the Rebbe's advice on the purchase of a forest, amounting to a very large sum of money. The Rebbe approved the transaction but demanded two per cent of the sum to help the bride. At first, the merchant hesitated, but in the end he turned over the money which our Rebbe then handed the poor man. A few days later, arrangements for the match were completed in the home and presence of the Rebbe.

Giving to the Poor, Jews and non-Jews Alike.

Once, when the Rebbe visited Máramaros County a woman came before him complaining that her cow had been stolen. When asked by the Rebbe on which day this happened, she answered, "Ten days ago." Added the Rebbe with a smile, "Nu, what do you want? I wasn't here then!" In the end, he took a handful of silver coins from his table, and asked that it be given her for the purchase of another cow.

Once a poor woman with a little boy came to the Rebbe

complaining that she did not own a cent and couldn't even buy her son a pair of shoes. The Rebbe took a handful of money from the table before him and told his aide to give it to her. The aide, surprised over the large sum, hesitated a bit. Said our Rebbe, (may his merit protect us) "You do not see the great pain this woman is in? Quick! Give her the money."

He also used to give money to non-Jews. When he met a non-Jew on the road collecting alms, he used to give some coins to one of the people present to hand to the non-Jew and would quote from the Talmud (Gitin 61a), "One supports the poor non-Jews as well as the poor Jews."

GIZELLA PERL

The following is one of the most remarkable documents and personal stories of the 20th century. Written by Gizella Perl, the daughter of a pious father and a mother ambitious for her seven children. She was born in Sziget in 1899.

What led me to her office on Park Avenue in New York City was not only her book, I Was a Doctor in Auschwitz, but also a desire to find out how she managed to become the first woman physician in an environment where "Women's Lib" had barely made its appearance. The story, graciously given to me, speaks for itself. There is little that I can, or want, to add except perhaps that Dr. Perl, at 80, has now reached her goal of moving to Israel, much to the regret of her many patients, some of whom were themselves survivors of the Holocaust. She told me that many of them will continue to see her in her new medical office in Israel. One can easily see why; for Gizella has always been more than just a doctor. She is a healer concerned with human beings, trying to help them in every way and whenever they are in need.

Her own life represents hope and faith in its highest form; it is an inspiration to all who are fortunate to meet her or read her story.

MY LIFE

It wasn't easy to break through the customs of a Jewish Orthodox family when, after graduating summa cum laude from the eight years of Gymnasium, I wanted to enter medical school and become a "Doctor." My mother was the liberal in the family — push all her seven children to a Dr. title — but my father was the stubborn, observant Jew. For weeks I fought for his permission to leave home but my father remained unconvinceable. Then, one evening with my prayer book in hand, I said, "Father, I swear by this prayer book I shall always remain a good Jew — wherever I shall go — just let me start the study of medicine . . ." A few days later, my father took me to the medical school in Budapest. I was studying diligently long hours with love. During my university years I got married and we went to Berlin for postgraduate studies, where we were working very seriously in our special fields, not seeing each other for many days . . .

Suddenly, Germany became a fearful country — the sky covered with dark clouds, the air filled with dark shadows of future tragedies . . . Friends and colleagues warned us to leave before it is too late — Hitler's voice shouted day and night . . . We returned to my home town — opened our offices . . . I remember the first day of my medical practice, I performed some small gynecological surgery — This was my first income. I ran with this money to an old Jewish bookshop asking for an unusual prayerbook. I found one of the rare printing on fine pergament paper; my father's initials of silver were added and I brought this prayer book to my father's room saying, "I give you back the prayer book with a new oath, I shall remain a good Jew forever!" When we traveled in the cattle wagons towards Auschwitz, my father kept my prayer book — his only possession, right over his heart — holding it as he went to the gas chambers.

Nine beautiful years we spent in my home town. Young brave doctors, achieving very soon moral and financial success. We started almost the first day to be active in Zionist work. There was no one field where we didn't participate as leaders for Zion, may it be Keren Kayemet, Keren Hayessod, Young Wizo — Chalutz movement, we were at the head with work and money. These were nine happy years . . . Medicine and Zionism made our life rich with joy.

Then came the time with deprivations of our soul and body — the sad days in the ghetto . . . to leave my beloved town . . . finally cattle wagons and Auschwitz — the brutal separation from parents — husband — child . . .

The sky was covered with flames in Auschwitz on our arrival — the air filled with stench of burning bodies and the SS officers gave us the taste of their murderous games with wild dogs and heavy whips.

In Auschwitz — and later in Bergen-Belsen — I worked with an unbelievable zeal to help my prison mates, to remain a Doctor. Here I learned from my daily experience about psychosomatic medicine. I didn't have chemicals for the agonizing pain nor bandages for the open prurient skin ulcers — I didn't have facilities to heal my people's suffering, but I had my convincing voice of hope, my convincing words of a better future — that one day the doors of this hell will be open, and we shall be free human beings again; just try not to feel the pain of the tortured body and soul, I told them stories — poems, parables to subdue their sufferings.

Being an obstetrician-gynecologist, my deepest unforgettable trauma in Auschwitz came from Dr. Mengele, the "Famous Murderer" Chief Physician in Auschwitz. Dr. Mengele played the most cruel games with human beings — especially with the pregnant women. I had to report to him every newly-arrived pregnant prisoner, with the promise that the women will be sent to better living quarters, with better food, and water. After 1-2 weeks, I realized that the pregnant women were sent to the experimental blocks where Mengele performed his sadistic experiments. There were no more

pregnant women reported! Every night I performed abor-
tions, premature babies, with my bare dirty fingers, saving
many, many lives. It was another "medicine" in Auschwitz.
Later, I was able to deliver many children here in America for
those very mothers aborted in Auschwitz.

In Bergen-Belsen, the Angel of Death was typhus. Dead
or dying human beings formed little mountains in the streets
— or agonizing, semi-conscious emaciated bodies lying in
the wooden cages waiting for the liberator, Death. Day and
night I worked, as one possessed, to help make the suffering
or death easier.

When the British Army liberated us, I was not only able
to be a "Healer," but a real Doctor again. I got a small hospital
in Bergen-Belsen, with some medical instruments and basic
drugs. After liberation, the typhus epidemic didn't just disappear; hungry, starving human beings started to eat without
limitations, just to fill again the stomach — and the Death
Angel was still taking its human sacrifice.

I cannot let die anyone — I have to save everyone! I didn't
care for sleep — I didn't care for food. I was just a Doctor
again, running from one bed to another — till I collapsed with
the typhus myself.

After a few months, I was strong enough to work with the
same fire, and then I got my cherished diploma from the
liberating British Army for my medical work in Bergen-
Belsen. In the last days in Bergen-Belsen I became an envied
hero. The Jewish Agency sent me a special certificate — for
an only woman — to appear in their office in Paris — because
they wanted me to go to the then Palestine. It was a great
honor — and luck — but then I realized, maybe in the first
conscious realization, that I am terribly alone, no parents, no
husband, no child — I am going alone to Zion — to our
dream . . .

In Paris, the Jewish leaders persuaded me, "You, Dr. Perl,
have now a greater duty. Go to America and tell the tragedy of
the Jewish People; speak about the Holocaust, help your

survivors." And I did. On a shaky Liberty ship travelling 4-5 days, I arrived in New York, not knowing the English language, not having any relatives, just some vaguely known people from my home town. And I started to tell my story, mainly for physicians' groups — going from one town to the other, from one hospital to the other, starting my speech always with the sentence, "I came here as an ambassador of six million dead," and continued in German, French, Hungarian, Yiddish, to speak about the horrors we suffered. The audience was crying and on my desk big money was placed.

It was Mrs. Eleanor Roosevelt, the late First Lady, who one day invited me to her New York apartment and told me, "Stop it, Dr. Perl, don't torture yourself — be a Doctor again." I did it! A great woman, a leader in the USA, Mrs. Hatty Grossman, brought me to Washington to meet the powerful Congressman, Sol Bloom. He listened to me, and in a few days introduced a Special Bill on my behalf to be admitted to the U.S.A. My status was as a "Visitor" only. Sol Bloom made it possible to have a hearing in the Judiciary Committee before the great members of the Committee. I can never, never forget how they were listening to my speech in broken English about the bestiality of the Nazi regime and the suffering of my people.

My Bill passed. I started to study for the N.Y. State Board Exam. I was sitting in the libraries, many times hungry but happy to go through my beloved medical books again. I was, at the same time, teaching new Doctors who were also studying for the State Board Exam, and this way I managed to survive a few months. One day, I was introduced to the famous gynecologist of the Mount Sinai Hospital, the late Doctor J.C. Rubin. He invited me to speak at the gynecological staff meeting — he made it possible to work at the gynecological clinic of the Mount Sinai Hospital. I was a real Doctor again. I opened my office. I did not have a bed to sleep in; I did not have a table to eat at, but I had my office in New York City.

The Mount Sinai opened its gynecological-obstetrical Department in a new modern building with an outstanding famous physician as Director, Dr. A. Guttmacher. He was not only my Chief, my friend, but my greatest helper! He organized a new clinic in our department, the vulvo-vaginitis clinic for research and teaching purposes, and made me the head of this clinic. I worked here daily each afternoon. I published many papers about my work. I had many presentations about new diagnostic methods, and new treatments in this field of gynecology.

My nights I spent on the delivery floor, to bring new life to this world. For one who had to destroy unborn lives to save mothers, it was the greatest blessing to deliver healthy, beautiful babies. It was an indescribable personal reward.

When the Mount Sinai medical school opened, I became one of the teaching staff, never being tired, never feeling too much work. I was a Doctor again!

My love for Israel became the second motive in my life, growing with every day. In the first ten years of my practice, I was the honorary Doctor for the "Israeli Student Organization" in New York, having many now famous people in my medical care, and never being tired or busy when I had to work, to speak for Israel.

My dream and my promise to my father is completely fulfilled. I am a Doctor and a Zionist with all my heart and brain.

THE REBBE AND THE HAZZAN

By Max Wohlberg

*The author of this very poignant story is
Professor of Hazzanut at the Cantors Institute
of the Jewish Theological Seminary of America.*

My great-great-grandfather, Ya'akov Wohlberg, left Warsaw
in order to escape conscription into military service and
came with his family to Hungary. His son, Isroel Shlomo,
became a Shochet and settled near Tokay. The latter had five
sons and two daughters. The daughters married businessmen. The oldest son, Leibish, became a Melamed and settled
in Palestine. Kopel was a Shochet and lived in Nagy Bánya.
Mendel immigrated to the United States and became a tailor.
Yosele (my grandfather) married Roize, the daughter of a
wealthy winegrower of Pátroha. Yehoshua, a *Menaker*, settled in Arad and died of blood poisoning at an early age.

As a young boy, my grandfather Yosele, as he was called
throughout his life, was given four *kreitzer* by his father and
sent to Cracow to study in the Yeshiva of Reb Shimon, the son
of the renowned Chatam Sofer.

After some years in Cracow, he returned home and became engaged and later married Roize, whose wealthy father
was a Hasid of the Rebbe of Sanz. For a while the young
couple lived with her parents. Then, Yosele, becoming rest-
less, traveled with his father-in-law to the Rebbe whom they
consulted about Yosele's future.

The Rebbe's advice to Yosele was, "Since you sing beau-

tifully and you are a *Talmid Chacham* and, above all, a man
of piety, you should become a Hazzan-Shochet." While Yosele was ready to accept the Rebbe's advice, his father-in-law
found it embarrassing to have his son-in-law serve as a
Shochet. The two returned home and resumed the previous
pattern of their lives. When an unusually cold, frosty winter,
however, ruined all the grapes in his father-in-law's vine-
yards, the latter again visited his Rebbe who repeated his
previous advice regarding Yosele.

Upon hearing of a vacancy for the position of Shochet in
the city of Ujhely, Yosele applied and was accepted. Life in
Ujhely, however, was not without problems. Roize found it
demeaning to be cast in the role of a Shochet's wife. Some
congregants were resentful of the richly furnished home of
the young couple, while the ultra pious looked askance at the
young Shochet's relatively modern garb.

At this time, the city of Szatmár was seeking a Shochet
and Yosele applied. He was interviewed by the Rav, R. Bin-
yamin Zev Mandelbaum, who also examined his *Chalaf*.
After thoroughly questioning the young candidate in relevant laws, the Rav was most favorably impressed by him. At
the request of the Rav, a small committee was assembled to
meet Yosele. Since the position of Hazzan was also currently
vacant someone asked Yosele to sing something and he ob-
liged. The committee was enchanted. It was decided to have a
congregational meeting take place during the following
week, when it was confidently expected the congregation
would approve the committee's recommendation.

At that time, there was in Szatmár a large contingent of
Hasidim of the Rebbe of Sziget. These men, wielding a great
deal of influence, found the young candidate a bit too modern, the Hasid of the wrong Rebbe and, furthermore, preferred
a Shochet hailing from Sziget.

Upon seeing the great affection shown Yosele and the
well nigh certainty of his engagement, the Hasidim of Sziget
hurriedly dispatched a delegation of two to their Rebbe for a

writ opposing the candidacy of Yosele Wohlberg being un-
worthy of this position. Two days later, the delegation returned with such a writ which they handed to the Rav.

The latter, while favoring Yosele, did not wish to an-
tagonize the Hasidim of the Rebbe of Sziget. In an untenable
situation, and not wishing to divulge the letter he had received, he tried to extricate himself by again asking to see
Yosele's Chalaf.

Yosele promptly brought his Chalaf to the Rav, who
minutely scrutinized it and finding no fault with it, an-
nounced, "Since it is not inconceivable that this Chalaf was
prepared by another individual, I will blunt it and ask you to
sharpen it to the appropriate degree." He thereupon struck
the sharp edge of the blade against the leg of the table.
Puzzled by the turn of events, Yosele took the damaged
Chalaf to his lodging and within two hours returned it to the
Rav, who again examined it and found it without blemish. "Is
this the same Chalaf that I examined before?" he asked. "It is
the only Chalaf I brought to Szatmár," answered Yosele.
Crestfallen, the Rav related to Yosele what had transpired
and expressing his regrets advised him to travel to Kisvárda
where a Hazzan-Shochet was currently needed. He, the Rav,
would be happy to recommend him in the highest terms.

Yosele was stunned. He expressed appreciation for the
recommendation, and promised to go to Kisvárda. What he
did not tell the Rav was that he decided to leave immediately
for Sziget and spend the Sabbath there.

After acquiring lodging and making arrangements for
meals, Yosele prepared himself for the Sabbath and after
services left for the Tish — the formal Sabbath meal presided
over by the Rebbe and attended by his devotees. Among the
crowd surrounding the long table stood Yosele joining in the
singing of Zemirot. Gradually, all eyes turned on the young
man, whose sweet voice could be heard above all the voices
of the assembled. A place was cleared for him on a bench at
the table. Soon the Rebbe turned to Yosele and asked him to

sing a Zemirah. Yosele sang with all his heart. When he
finished there was complete silence in the hall. Then the
Rebbe spoke and all bent forward in order not to miss a
syllable. Enthusiastic singing followed. Then the Rebbe
called to Yosele, asked him where he had studied, where he
lived and his name. When Yosele, now seated near the Rebbe,
answered all questions, the Rebbe as if looking in the distance, remained silent for awhile, then said to him softly,
"Come to see me tomorrow after *Havdalah*."

At the conclusion of the Sabbath, the Gabbay asked
Yosele to be the first to enter the Rebbe's private reception
room. Seated at his table, his head bowed, the Rebbe after
some silence lifted his head and gently addressed the young
man standing before him, "Reb Yosele, as you see by my
white beard, it is an old man speaking to you and asking for
your forgiveness. I was misled, and I sinned against you.
Please say you forgive me because I cannot live in peace
knowing that I have wronged an innocent man. In the years
left to me I will be more careful." The Rebbe stretched out his
hand across the table. Yosele kissed it and there were tears in
the eyes of both men.

The position in Szatmár was filled with dispatch and
although Yosele received, within the next weeks, a number of
tempting offers he accepted the position in Kisvárda where
he hoped to live in peace and rear a family. He held that
position until he passed away 45 years later.

He was revered by his community and much loved by his
congregation. Although the ultra pious criticized him for
subscribing to German and Hungarian newspapers, they
would only eat the meat of animals slaughtered by him. He
and his wife, Roizele, became the parents of six sons and
three daughters. The latter married merchants. Those of their
offspring who survived the Holocaust settled either in the
United States or in Israel.

The oldest son, Baruch, considered by the family as a

renegade, left for the United States where, to the best of my knowledge, he became a Reform rabbi. Kopel was sickly and passed away early. Yehoshua Beirach, (the last name, similar to Baruch, was added in an attempt to confuse the authorities regarding possible recruitment for military service) was the proprietor of a general store. Asher, who reportedly had the most beautiful voice in the family, became Hazzan-Shochet in Hadház, where he sired ten children.

Yirmiyahu (my father), was a brilliant and charming man. He was a fine scholar, writing beautifully in Hebrew, Yiddish, Hungarian and German, and possessed a sweet voice. He passed away at the age of 32.

Abraham Yitzchak, the youngest, became a "professional" Hazzan. He had an excellent coloratura, a phenomenal falsetto and held positions in Budapest and Brooklyn, New York. It may serve as an odd postcript to add that while my father became a Yeshiva student in Sziget, my brothers and I were Yeshiva students in Szatmár.

HASIDIC MELODIES

Since recorded history began, the religious heritage
of the Jewish people included song and dance.
They were living expressions of their faith in the
Almighty and their everpresent hope in a better
future. When Hasidism came upon the scene in the
18th century, an important part of its life style was
singing and dancing. The Rabbis from the House of
Vishnitz, so very active in our Carpathian mountain region, were particularly famous for their fine
voices and melodious tunes. They could trace their
love for music to Rabbi Jacob Kopel of Kolomea,
Galicia, the father of their dynasty, for he had been
the Hazzan of Rabbi Israel Ba'al Shem Tov,
the Founder of Hasidism.

On the next few pages the reader will find five
melodies chosen with the help of Hazzanim V.
Pasternak, A. Weisser and J. Malovany. Some of the
transcripts were prepared by J. Gordon and
M. Kushner, both students at the Cantors Institute
of the Jewish Theological Seminary of America.
The first two, "Vizamrun Loch" and "Vosik," are
from the Sabbath Liturgy and may be found in
Velvel Pasternak's Songs of the Chassidim, II,
(New York: Bloch Publishing Company 1971), p. 55
and 74. The third, "Lebedik Freylakh," transposed
from No. 4 of Vishnitzer Records, Bne Brak, Israel,
may be freely translated as follows:

Lively, happy, endlessly joyful
Eternally you are holy, People of Israel

1. Despite your pains and tears
   You must always remain joyous
   Though beaten, chased and persecuted
   Exiled through the endless years.
   Still, you did not lose your faith
   For Talis and T'filin are Thy life's armor.
   Impenetrable faith in your God
   Ties you to your loving Almighty.

Lively, happy, endlessly joyful, etc.

2. Fiery tongues swallow you
   Isles of tears explode you
   Still your soul you lift with joy
   At no time did you bow down
   Even when they stretched you on the altar
   For you always sang out aloud.
   Hear, O Israel, the Lord is One.

*The fourth piece, "Veyeda Kol Po'ul" is from the High
Holy Days liturgy and is taken from M. Eisikovits' Songs of
the Martyrs, Hassidic Melodies of Maramures,
(New York: Sepher Hermon Press, 1980), p. 6 ff.
The fifth tune, "Wedding Melody," while originally of
Vishnitz, is now sung by many Hasidic groups.
It is published in Otzar ha-Chasidut, comp.
André Hajdu, (Jerusalem: ha-Machon ha-Yisraeli
le-Musika ha-Datit, 1974), p. 95.*

VIZAMRUN LOCH

Vishnitz

And sing melodic hymns of praise –
Jerusalem, city of beauty.

וִיזַמְּרוּן לָךְ שִׁירִין וְרַחֲשִׁין,
בִּירוּשְׁלֵם קַרְתָּא דְּשַׁפְרַיָּא.

VOSIK

God bestow your mercy
and have pity upon the son of your beloved.
I have long yearned to behold
the glory of your strength.
These are the desires of my heart. Have mercy
and turn not away from us.

יק יֶהֱמוּ נָא רַחֲמֶיךָ
יסָה נָא עַל בֶּן אֲהוּבֶךָ
זֶה כַּמָה נִכְסוֹף נִכְסַפְתִּי
יאוֹת בְּתִפְאֶרֶת עֻזֶּךָ
ה חָמְדָה לִבִּי וְחוּסָה נָא
ל תִּתְעַלֵּם.

LEBEDIK FRELAKH

Le - be - dik lus- tik frey-lakh on a tsol to-mid bist du hey-lig folk Yis-

roel mit 1.day-ne shmer-tsn dayn ge veyn to-mid mizt du frey-lakh zayn
2.fay-er tsing-en shling-en dikh tre-rn inz-len pla-tsn dikh

khotch men yogt khotch men rogt un shlogt khotch in go-lus
dayn n'- sho-me hoybst du oyf mit freyd keyn mol host du

van-derst du shoyn vorn ____ dokh host du dayn
dikh nit ge- boi-gn ____ a - fi-le az men hot dikh oy-fn miz

gloy-bn nit far lorn ____ vayl tal-is un tfi-ln iz dokh dayn
bey-akh oys-ge tsoi-gn ____ vayl to-mid du shrayst nor to-mid du

leb-ns pan-ser kla-mert dikh in dayn li-bn Got
singst nor shma Yis-

FINE

a ha ha ha ha ha Tra - la
ro-el ha shem e ── khod

la-la la-la la etc. ____

D.S. AL FINE

M. KUSHNER

וְיֵדַע כָּל פָּעוּל

VEYEIDA KOL PO'UL

From the High Holy Days Liturgy

Ve-yei-da kol po-ul ki a-to pe-al-toi ve-
yo — vin kol ye-tzur ki a-to ye-tzar-toi. Ve-
yei-da kol po-ul ki a-to pe-al-toi ve- yo-vin kol ye-tzur ki a-to ye-tzar-toi.

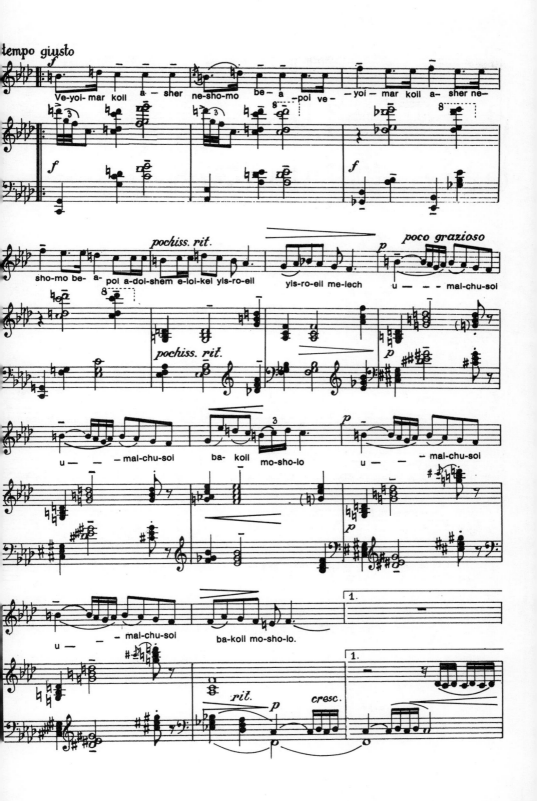

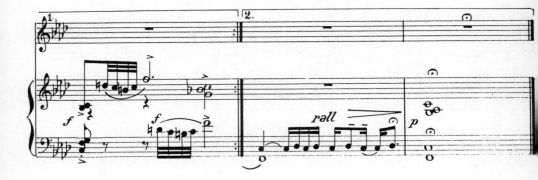

וידע כל פעול

וְיֵדַע כָּל פָּעוּל כִּי אַתָּה פְעַלְתּוֹ
וְיָבִין כָּל יְצוּר כִּי אַתָּה יְצַרְתּוֹ
וְיֹאמַר כֹּל אֲשֶׁר נְשָׁמָה בְאַפּוֹ
יי אֱלֹקֵי יִשְׂרָאֵל מֶלֶךְ
וּמַלְכוּתוֹ בַּכֹּל מָשָׁלָה

Wedding melody

APPENDIX

STATISTICS
GLOSSARIES
BIBLIOGRAPHY

STATISTICS

POPULATION STATISTICS OF SUBCARPATHIAN RUTHENIA DURING THE 19th & 20th CENTURIES*

1828

COUNTY	MARKETS	VILLAGES	GENERAL POPULATION	JEWISH
Ung	5	206	84,251	4,904
Bereg	9	258	91,562	4,146
Máramaros	5	136	120,852	6,064
Ugocsa	6	65	40,645	1,216
Totals	25	665	337,310	16,330

JEWISH POPULATION

1857	1870	1900	1910
45,216	64,903	112,400	128,791

JEWISH PERCENTAGE

	1880	1890	1900	1910
Ung	13.0	11.5	11.0	10.0
Bereg	13.5	13.6	14.0	14.2
Máramaros	14.7	16.8	18.1	18.4
Ugocsa	12.0	12.5	12.7	12.9

*Some of the figures which are approximate were extracted from *KARPA-TORUS* p. 117 f., and subject articles in the *ENCYCLOPAEDIA JUDAICA*.

RELIGIOUS AFFILIATION 1910

	ROMAN CATHOLICS	GREEK	PROTESTANTS	JEWS	OTHERS
Ung	34,549	89,149	20,092	17,587	712
Bereg	23,003	117,435	61,106	33,660	1,407
Máramaros	26,204	254,215	9,646	65,694	1,946
Ugocsa	8,173	57,550	14,002	11,850	180
Totals	91,929	518,349	104,846	128,791	4245

NUMBER AND PERCENTAGE OF JEWS IN MAJOR CITIES

1930

MUNKÁCS	11,313	43%
SZIGET	10,609	38%
UNGVÁR	7,357	33%
BEREGSZÁSZ	5,680	29%
HUSZT	4,821	16%
KÖRÖSMEZÖ	1,435	12%

LOSSES OF HUNGARIAN JEWRY*

Specifications:	Budapest	Province	Total	Lost Territory	Total
ACCORDING TO 1941 CENSUS:					
1. Of the Jewish faith	184,453	216,528	400,981	324,026	725,007
Non-Jews considered as Jews	62,350	27,290	89,640	10,360	100,000
Total Number of Jews	246,803	243,818	490,621	334,386	825,007
LOSS PRIOR TO GERMAN OCCUPATION:					
2. Labor service-men	12,350	12,500	24,850	17,150	42,000
Deported foreign Jews (July, 1941)	3,000	2,000	5,000	15,000	20,000
Ujvidék [Novisad] massacre (January, 1942)				1,000	1,000
Total:	15,350	14,500	29,850	33,150	63,000
No. of Jews on March 19,1944	231,453	229,318	460,771	301,236	762,007
DURING GERMAN OCCUPATION:					
Deported, killed, deceased	105,453	222,318	327,771	290,236	618,007
Fled abroad	2,000	1,000	3,000	2,000	5,000
Total:	107,453	223,318	330,771	292,236	623,007
Remnant	124,000	6,000	130,000	9,000	139,000
3. Liberated: As labor-service men on Hungarian territory.	5,000	6,000	11,000	9,000	20,000
In Budapest	119,000	—	119,000	—	119,000
NO. OF JEWS AT LIBERATION:					
4. Returned from deportation up to the end of 1945	20,000	40,000	60,000	56,000	116,500
No. of Jews on 12/31/45	144,000	47,000	191,000	65,500	255,500
Jewry's loss:	102,803	196,818	299,621	268,886	569,507

*Chart of World Jewish Congress, Hungarian Section as printed in:
Randolph L. Braham, *The Hungarian Labor Service System, 1939-1945*, (New York: 1977), p. 120.

GLOSSARY

AJDC	American Joint Distribution Committee, known for short as JOINT. American-Jewish Relief Organization, operating continuously since 1914.
ARA	American Relief Administration, organized after World War I to aid victims in Europe.
ASHKENAZIM	Jews originating from Germany and Northern France.
BENSH LICHT	Blessing the Sabbath and Holiday candles.
BESHT	Initials of Baal Shem Tov (Master of Good Name). Rabbi Israel ben Eliezer, Father of Hasidism (1700-1760).
BET DIN	Rabbinical Court.
BET MIDRASH	House of Study and Worship.
CHALAF	Shochet's knife.
CHEDER	Traditional Jewish elementary school.
DAYAN	Judge, member of rabbinical court.
D.P.	Displaced person.
ECHA	(How), opening word of Biblical Book of Lamentations.
GABBAY	Assistant to Rebbe.
G.I.	Government Issue. Nickname of the American soldier during World War II.
HAGANAH	Organization for Jewish Self-Defense in Palestine.
HALACHAH	Jewish Law.
HASIDISM	Religious movement originating with the Besht in the 18th century.
HASIDUT	Hasidic ideology.
HAVDALAH	Ceremony at conclusion of Shabbat.
HAZZAN	Cantor.
JDC	See AJDC.
JOINT	See AJDC.
JWB	Also NJWB, initials for National Jewish Welfare Board, agency serving the religious needs of Jewish military personnel.

KABBALAH	Jewish mysticism.
KEST	Free board and lodging to enable a newly-wed husband to pursue his religious studies.
KOLEL	Group of Jews from European countries living in the Holy Land, who received financial support from their former communities.
KOSHER	Food prepared according to the dietary laws.
MAGYAR	Hungarian.
MELAMED	Teacher of children.
MENAKER	Porger: Person who makes a slaughtered animal ritually clean by removing the forbidden fat and veins.
MEZUZAH	Biblical parchment placed at the doorpost of Jewish home.
MINYAN	A group of ten male adult Jews, required for communal worship.
MITNAGDIM	Opponents: those opposed to Hasidism.
MITZVAH	Religious commandment.
MOHEL	Person who performs the rite of circumcision.
NEOLOG	Jewish group in Hungary that favored liberal religious ideas as opposed to Orthodoxy.
NUMERUS CLAUSUS	Restricted number: anti-Semitic legislation denying Jews access to higher education.
ODA	Opportunity Development Association, organization formed during the 1970's to develop the Williamsburg section of Brooklyn, New York.
ORTHODOX	Adherent of strict traditional Judaism.
PARNAS	Provider: title of community leader.
RABBI	Jewish clergyman; also man of learning.
RAV	See: Rabbi.
REBBE	Hasidic rabbi.

ROSH HASHANAH	New Year.
SABBA KADISHA	Holy Old Man: honorific applied to Rabbi Israel, the Vishnitzer Rebbe (1860-1936).
SAMBATYON	Legendary river that throws stones on weekdays and rests on the Sabbath.
SELICHOT	Penitential prayers.
SEPHARDIM	Jews originating from Spain. Also applied to Ashkenazic Jews who followed the Lurianic liturgy.
SHAEF	Supreme Headquarters Allied Expeditionary Forces in World War II.
SHEHECHEYANU	Benediction of Thanksgiving.
SHEMA	Hear. Opening word of Declaration of Faith: Hear, O Israel, the Lord our God, the Lord is One.
SHOCHET	Ritual slaughterer.
SHOLEM ALEICHEM	Pen name of Solomon Rabinowitz (1859-1916), famous Yiddish writer.
SHULCHAN ARUCH	"Set table": The Code of Jewish Laws.
SS	Schutzstaffel: Nazi paramilitary organization.
STATUS QUO	"As before": designation of Hungarian Jewish congregations that did not join either the Orthodox or the Neolog group.
TALMUD TORAH	Teaching the Jewish way of life.
TORAH	Five books of Moses; body of Jewish teachings.
TOVIM	(Good Ones), community leaders.
TZADDIK	Righteous Man; Hasidic leader.
UNRRA	United Nations Relief and Rehabilitation Administration, organization active during and after World War II.
VAAD HATZALAH	Rabbinical Relief and Rescue Organization, active from 1939 to 1948.
YESHIVAH	Talmudic academy.
ZECHOR BRIT	"Remember the Covenant": opening words of a penitential prayer.
ZEMIROT	Sabbath songs.

GLOSSARY OF GEOGRAPHICAL TERMS

BEREGSZÁSZ (H); Berehovo (C); Beregovo (R).

CLUJ (R); Klausenburg (G); Kolozsvár (H).

DELATYN (P); Delyatin (R).

HUSZT (H); Chust (C); Khust (R).

KÖRÖSMEZÖ (H); Jasina (C); Yasinya (R).

KOLOMEA (G); Kolomyja (P); Kolomyya (R).

MUNKÁCS (H); Mukacevo (C); Mukachevo (R).

NAGYSZÖLLÖS (H); Sevlus or Sevljus (C); Sevlyush (R).

PRESSBURG (G); Bratislava (C); Pozsony (H).

RAHO (H); Rachov (C); Rakhov (R).

SZATMÁR (H); Satu-Mare (Rum); Satmar (Yid).

SZIGET or MÁRAMAROSSZIGET (H); Sighet (Rum).

UNGVÁR (H); Uzhorod (C); Uzhgorod (R).

VISHNITZ (G); Vijnita (Rum); Vishnitsa (R).

Abbreviations:

C	Czech
G	German
H	Hungarian
P	Polish
Rum	Rumanian
R	Russian
Y	Yiddish

Source: The Columbia Lippincott Gazetteer of the World, ed. Leon E. Seltzer, New York 1952.

BIBLIOGRAPHY

Alfasi, Isaac
>
> *Tiferet she-be-malchut*, Tel Aviv: Ariel, 1961.

Bauer, Yehuda
>
> *Flight and Rescue: Brichah*, New York: Random House, 1970.
>
> *My Brother's Keeper*: A History of the American Joint Distribution Committee 1929-1939, Philadelphia: Jewish Publication Society, 1974.
>
> "The Holocaust and the Struggle of the Yishuv as Factors in the Establishment of the State of Israel," *Holocaust and Rebirth*, Jerusalem: Yad Vashem, 1974.

Ben-Amos, Dan and Mintz, Jerome R., eds.
>
> *In Praise of the Baal Shem Tov (Shivche Ha-Besht)*, The Earliest Collection of Legends about the Founder of Hasidism, Bloomington: Indiana University Press, 1970.

Ben-Menachem, Naphtali
>
> *Mi-Sifrut Israel be-Hungaria*, Jerusalem: Kiryat Sefer, 1958.

Bernstein, Philip S.
>
> *Rabbis at War: The CANRA Story*, Waltham: American Jewish Historical Society, 1971.

Bikel, Shlomo
>
> "Der Szigeter Sholom Aleichem," *Máramarossziget*, Tel Aviv, July 1962.

Braham, Randolph L.
>
> *The Politics of Genocide, The Holocaust in Hungary*, Vol. 1 & 2, New York: Columbia University Press, 1981.

Czechoslovakia, see: Jews of Czechoslovakia

Danzig, Hillel
>
> *Be-Tzel Susim*. Story of a Labor Batallion of Hunga-

rian Jews at the Russian Front, Tel Aviv: ha-Kibbutz ha-Meuchad, 1976.

Dicker, Herman
"The US Army and Jewish Displaced Persons," *Chicago Jewish Forum*, (Summer 1961) Vol. XIX, No. 4.
Wanderers and Settlers, A Century of Jewish Life in China and Japan, New York: Twayne Publishers, 1962.
A Jewish Family Trail, The Dickers and Their Mates, New York: Express Printing Company, 1977.

Encyclopaedia of the Jewish Diaspora-Karpatorus, Vol. VII, ed. Yehuda Erez, Tel Aviv: 1959.

Fleischmann, Gustave
"Religious Life and Organizations," *Czechoslovakia*, Vol. I, p. 311 ff.

Friedmann, Armin H.
Major Aspects of Yeshiva Education in Hungary, Ph.D. Dissertation, Yeshiva University, New York: 1971.

Fuchs, Abraham
Hungarian Yeshivot, From Grandeur to Holocaust, Jerusalem: 1978.

Gottlieb, Hirsch Leib
Lider fun mein Leben, Satmar, Romania: J. Wieder's Buchdruckerei, 1933.

Greenwald Leopold
Matzevet Kodesh, New York: Hadar Linotyping and Publishing Company, 1952.

Grossmann, Kurt R.
The Jewish Displaced Persons Problem, New York: World Jewish Congress, 1951.
"Refugees to and from Czechoslovakia," *Czechoslovakia*, Tel. II, p. 565 f.

Hoffman, Chaim
"Displaced Persons," *Encyclopaedia Judaica*, Jerusalem: Macmillan Company, 1971, Vol. 6, p. 75 ff.

Hungarian-Jewish Studies, ed. Randolph L. Braham, Vol. I to III, New York: World Federation of Hungarian Jews, 1966-1973.

Jews of Czechoslovakia, The, Vol. I & II, Philadelphia: The Jewish Publication Society of America; New York: Society for the History of Czechoslovak Jews, 1968-1971.

Karpatorus, see: Encyclopaedia of the Jewish Diaspora-Karpatorus.

Katzburg, Nathaniel
> "Hungarian Jewry in Modern Times," *Studies*, Vol. I, p. 137 ff.

Klein, Bernard
> "Hungarian Politics and the Jewish Question in the Inter-War Period," *Jewish Social Studies*, (April 1966) Vol. XXVIII, No. 2, p. 79 ff.

Klein, Isaac
> *A Guide to Jewish Religious Practice*, New York: The Jewish Theological Seminary of America, 1978.

Kranzler, George
> *Williamsburg: A Jewish Community in Transition*, New York: Feldheim, 1961.

Lamm, Norman
> "The Ideology of the Neturei Karta According to the Satmarer Version," *Tradition*, (Fall, 1971) Vol. XII, No.2 , p.38 ff.

László, Ernö
> "Hungary's Jewry, a Demographic Overview, 1918-1945," *Studies*, Vol. II, p. 137 ff.

Lavender, Abraham, D. ed.
> *A Coat of Many Colors, Jewish Subcommunities in the United States*, Westport, Connecticut: Greenwood Press, 1977.

Magocsi, Paul Robert
> *The Shaping of a National Identity, Subcarpathian Rus*, 1848-1948, Cambridge: Harvard University Press, 1978.

Mahler, Raphael
A History of Modern Jewry, London: Vallentine, Mitchell, 1971
Máramarossziget: Periodical published by the "Irgun Máramarossziget B'Israel" Tel Aviv.
Marton, Ernest
"The Family tree of Hungarian Jewry," Studies, Vol. I, p. 1 ff.
Mintz, Jerome R.
Legends of the Hasidim, Chicago: University of Chicago Press, 1968.
Nadich, Judah
Eisenhower and the Jews, New York: Twayne Publishers, 1953.
Parvin, J. L. and Schreiber, Perez, eds.
Di Yidishe Landsmanshaften fun New York, New York: Works Progress Administration, 1938.
Perl, Gizella
I was a Doctor in Auschwitz, New York: International Universities Press, 1948.
Poll, Solomon
The Hasidic Community of Williamsburg, New York: Free Press of Glencoe, 1962.
"The Role of Yiddish in American Ultra-Orthodox and Hasidic Communities," Yivo Annual of Jewish Social Science, Vol. XIII, (New York: 1965) p. 125 ff.
Rabinowicz, Aharon Moshe K.
"The Jewish Minority," Czechoslovakia, Vol. I, p. 155 ff.
"The Jewish Party," Ibid., Vol. II, p. 253 ff.
Reinharz, Shimon
"Pirke Havai," Karpatorus, p. 302 ff.
Reitlinger, Gerald
The Final Solution, London: Valentine, Mitchell, 1968.
Rothkirchen, Livia
"Deep-Rooted yet Alien: Some Aspects of the History

of the Jews in Subcarpathian Ruthenia," *Yad Vashem Studies*, Vol. XII, Jerusalem: Yad Vashem, 1977, p. 147 ff.

Rothschild, Joseph
  East Central Europe between the Two World Wars, Seattle: University of Washington Press, 1974

Rubin, Israel
  Satmar, An Island in the City, Chicago: Quadrangle Books, 1972.

Schwartz, Yehuda
  Toldot ha-Kehilot be-Transylvania, Hadera, Israel: 1976.

Sole, Aryeh
  "Modern Hebrew Education in Subcarpathian Ruthenia," *Czechoslovakia*, Vol. II, p. 401 ff.
  "Subcarpathian Ruthenia 1918-1938," *Ibid.*, Vol. I, p. 125 ff.

Spiegel, Yehuda
  "Ungvár," *Arim ve-Imahot be-Yisrael*, Vol. IV, ed. Y.L. Maimon, Jerusalem: Mosad Harav Kook, 1950. p. 5 ff.

Studies, see Hungarian-Jewish Studies.

Teitelbaum, Yoel
  Va-yoel Moshe, Brooklyn: "Jerusalem", 1959.
  Kunteres al ha-Geulah ve-al ha-Temurah, Brooklyn; Sender Deutsch Publisher, 1967.

Ussoskin, Moshe
  Struggle for Survival, Jerusalem: Academic Press, 1975.

Vágó, Béla
  "The Destruction of the Jews of Transylvania," *Studies*, Vol. I, p. 171 ff.
  "Germany and the Jewish Policy of the Kállay Government," *Ibid.*, Vol. II, p. 183 ff.

Végházi, István
  "The Role of Jewry in the Economic Life of Hungary," *Studies*, Vol. II, p. 70 ff.

Weinberger, Bernard

"Confessions of an Orthodox Rabbi or a Tale of Three Bridges," *Jewish Life*, Vol. I, No. 1 (Fall 1975), p. 15 ff.
"The Growing Rate of Divorce in Orthodox Jewish Life," *Ibid.*, Vol. I, No. 3, (Spring 1976), p. 9 ff.
"Satmar and Lubavitch: The Dynamics of a Disagreement," *Ibid.*, Vol. II, No. 2-3, (Fall-Winter 1977-78), p. 55 ff.

Weingarten, Samuel Hakohen

"Le-Korot ha-Yehudim be-Karpatorus," *Karpatorus*, p. 21 ff.
"Munkács," *Arim ve-Imahot be-Yisrael*, ed. Y. L. Fishman, Vol. I, Jerusalem: Mosad Harav Kook, 1946, p. 345 ff.

Weiss-Halivni, David

Meqorot Umesorot, Vol. I, Tel Aviv: Dvir, 1968; Vol. II, New York: Jewish Theological Seminary of America, 1975.
"Contemporary Methods of the Study of the Talmud," *Journal of Jewish Studies*, Vol. XXX, No. 2, (Autumn 1979), p. 192 ff.

Wiesel, Eli

Night, London: MacGibbon and Kee, 1960.
A Bibliography, comp. Mollie Abramowitz, Metuchen, N.J.: Scarecrow Press, 1974.
Confronting the Holocaust: The Impact of Elie Wiesel, ed. A. H. Rosenfeld and I. Greenberg, Bloomington: Indiana University Press, 1978.

INDEX